aquarium STYLE

aquarium
STYLE

IMAGINATIVE IDEAS FOR CREATING
DREAM HOMES FOR FISH

Matthew Christian

A QUARTO BOOK
Copyright © 2000 Quarto Inc.

First edition for the United States, its territories
and dependencies and Canada
published in 2000 by
Barron's Educational Series, Inc.

All inquiries should be addressed to:
Barron's Educational Series, Inc.
250 Wireless Boulevard
Hauppauge, NY 11788
http://www.barronseduc.com

Library of Congress Cataloging-in-Publication
Data No. 99-69840

ISBN 0-7641-5280-7

QUAR.QUA

Conceived, designed, and produced by
Quarto Publishing
6 Blundell Street
London N7 9BH

Editor Judith Samuelson
Art Editor Michelle Stamp
Copy Editor Geoff Barker
Designer Tanya Devonshire-Jones
Photographer Paul Forrester and Colin Bowling
Illustrator Michelle Stamp
Indexer Dorothy Frame

Art Director Moira Clinch
Publisher Piers Spence

Publisher's Note
Always check with your aquarium store on the
correct handling of aquarium fish and the
appropriate use of the commercial products
used in this book.

All statements, information, and advice given in
this book are believed to be accurate. However,
neither the author, copyright holder, nor
publisher accepts any legal liability for errors or
omissions.

Manufactured by Regent Publishing Services,
Hong Kong.
Printed by Leefung-Asco Printers Ltd, China

9 8 7 6 5 4 3 2 1

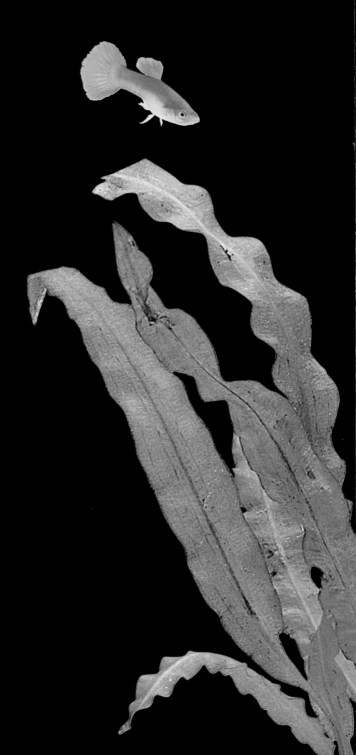

contents

setting up a healthy
AQUARIUM

Gravel, sand, and stones must be carefully washed in plenty of clean water.

Water-testing kits are available to test the specific gravity of the water. This is essential for providing the right environment for your fish. Check with your aquarium store for details on using these products.

Setting up an aquarium is a little like creating a miniature biosphere. There are many things that an aquarium requires, and every effort must be made to get the conditions just right.

PLANNING
Before you set up your tank, you should plan every stage in the process, since it will be harder to make changes later.

First, a strong and steady base is needed for the aquarium, as a tank full of water is an extremely heavy. Consult your aquarium store on the wide range of tanks available. Once you have found a suitable cabinet, you will need a thick sheet of polystyrene cut to the width and depth of the tank and placed under the base. This is vital, since the tank can crack if the base is not level.

CLEANLINESS
The first rule of thumb when setting up your aquarium is cleanliness. Be sure to clean everything thoroughly to remove any dust, loose chippings, dirt, pollutants, or chemicals.

Do not use any kind of detergent, since this can end up in the aquarium water and kill your fish. If you suspect your tank or props have been washed with detergent, soak in clean water for at least a day, then rinse under running water for at least 30 minutes, or in several changes of water.

To rinse gravel, sand, glass pebbles, or rocks, take a few handfuls of the material and put it in a bucket. Under running water, swirl this around and then pour out the water, holding back the gravel with your hands. Repeat this at least ten times until the water runs out clear.

Once you have set up your aquarium, you need to keep levels of algae and debris on the inside of your tank to a minimum. Algae is a small plant that grows in the water due to the increased amount of light in your aquarium. Use a suitable scraper to push it off the glass. You can also use a capture net to collect waste materials, as well as for separating live fish or removing dead fish.

FILTRATION
Before you add the gravel to the tank, you must put down your sub-gravel filter. A filter helps keep your aquarium water clear of any debris, such as food or fish droppings, as it sucks these gently down to the base of the tank and into the gravel.

Your filter needs to be as close to the size of your tank base as possible, so that it fits snugly over the base.

Position the air pump tube in the rear corner of the filter in the specially provided hole. The tube uses the pressure from the air pump to draw the water down through the gravel, which helps to purify it before sucking it up the pipe and redistributing it into the top half of the tank.

Cover the filter with a flat layer of gravel or other base medium, no less than 2 in (5cm) deep. Gently bank up the base layer toward the rear of the tank.

HEATING
To keep your tank at a regular temperature in which your fish will thrive, you will need a heater and thermostat. The thermostat will keep the water at a constant temperature and should be set to 77°F/25°C for the best conditions. Some fish may need different settings, so always check at your aquarium store when buying fish.

Once you have set up the heating system, you can leave it to work automatically. However, it is vital to never turn the power on while there is no water in the tank, and check the water level is always above the top of the heater, otherwise it will overheat and crack.

To help regulate the tank temperature, stick a liquid crystal thermometer to the outside of your tank. If the water temperature falls too low, tropical fish will feel the chill and be susceptible to infection. If the water temperature rises too high, then the water will lose oxygen and your fish may suffocate.

LIGHTING
As your tank will be kept indoors, artificial light is required to keep your fish and plants healthy.

Aquarium lighting comes in the form of a miniature fluorescent tube which sits in your tank lid. These tubes produce very little excess heat, unlike an ordinary light bulb, so the temperature of your tank is not greatly affected.

There are many different types of aquarium lighting. The best light for plant and fish growth is the grolux system as it enhances the color of your fish and stimulates plant growth.

It is important that all wires and cords are properly grounded and kept well above the water level, preferably outside the tank. The tank's hood will help keep the wires out of view and away from any water that is splashed upwards by the pump. Check with your aquarium store on the correct use of lighting devices.

Real or synthetic bogwood provides your fish with safe places to hide.

There are many ways of providing shelter for your fish. Urns make an effective prop, but must be cleaned well before use.

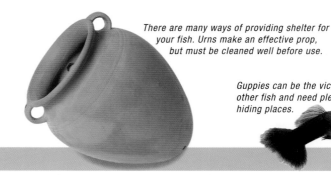

Guppies can be the victims of other fish and need plenty of hiding places.

AERATION

Fish breathe by using oxygen that has dissolved in water. They then excrete carbon dioxide back into the water. Decaying food and plant life adds yet more carbon dioxide to the water, and if these levels outweigh the amount of oxygen in the water, your fish will suffocate.

To avoid this, it is important that you use an air pump to help push air through the water. This increases the level of dissolved oxygen in the water, removes excess carbon dioxide, helps the water circulate, prevents cold spots, and re-creates the currents found in streams and the ocean.

Air pumps use a submerged diffuser to pump air through a filter and release a stream of tiny bubbles into the water. The best pump for most household aquariums is a vibratory pump, which is both economical and easy to install. It needs little maintenance. If it does clog up, you can use a pipe cleaner or a knitting needle to dislodge any trapped residue. Fit the air pump to the top of the tube that runs from the sub-gravel filter. This will allow it to sit just below the waterline, and its air supply tube can sit above the water level to provide the necessary airflow.

SHADE AND HIDING PLACES

Your fish need shade and hiding places so they can escape from the glare of the aquarium light and other fish. This is always something that deserves special consideration when designing your tank. Usually, this shade and shelter comes from plants, rocks, and wood, but if none of these are present, then you will have to provide alternative safe places for your fish. If you are using rocks, create shade and shelter by making little alcoves between the rocks or pebbles. Irregular shapes in wood and branches can give shelter to smaller fish.

Plants naturally provide shade and escape routes between their stems and leaves. Large plants with broad leaves, such as Arrowhead, Sword Plants, or Giant Indian Water Stars are the best types to provide shade, whereas bushy plants, such as Myriophyllum, Cabomba, or Water Milfoil are ideal for making natural hiding places.

CHOOSING YOUR TANK

Before deciding on what size tank you want to buy, it is important to decide where in the home you want to keep it and what you plan to put into it.

LOCATION

First of all you need to find a place away from drafts and windows, since sunlight will increase the rate at which algae grows and also the temperature of the tank. The tank needs to be either on a cabinet that will withstand the weight of the filled tank or on a solid piece of furniture. Alcoves or disused fireplaces can be especially effective places to keep an aquarium.

Your tank must be kept out of busy hallways so that the fish aren't knocked or disturbed. Another issue to bear in mind is that you will need a power supply to power the heater, light, and air pump.

DIMENSIONS

Once you have found the location for your tank, measure the space available and see what size tank will fit—there is no point buying a large tank if you only have a small space in which to fit it. Once you know how much space you have, consider what kind of design you plan on having

in your aquarium. All the designs in this book can be adapted to fit different tanks; take care to match the proportions of the scenery to the shape of the tank.

TANK SIZE

As a general rule, try to buy the biggest tank you can afford and that you can fit into your home. The larger the tank, the more stable the water quality and temperature will be, which will cause the least amount of stress to your fish. Whatever size tank you have, always take care not to overstock with fish, since this will inhibit and harm them.

Piranhas are carnivorous and are best kept in a single species tank.

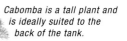

Shark Catfish can be very aggressive to other species.

Cabomba is a tall plant and is ideally suited to the back of the tank.

Lobelia looks great at the front of the tank.

Plastic fern plants are a versatile, maintenance-free option.

SELECTING COMPATIBLE AQUATIC LIFE

Choosing the right fish is vital if you want to keep a well-stocked and happy aquarium. Grouping fish with compatible companions will ensure safety for all the inhabitants of the tank. Small fish, such as Guppies or Tetras, must not be housed with larger or more aggressive fish, such as large Angelfish.

AGGRESSIVE FISH

Some fish are aggressive towards other, smaller breeds of fish or even towards each other if kept in large numbers. Some fish, such as the notorious Piranha, are carnivorous and aggressive. Other species are peaceful when kept alone or in a couple, but turn into a fighting force if grouped in shoals. Oscars of any description will quickly bully, peck, and finally eat other

breeds of fish. Therefore, if you like the striking colors and habits of the Oscar, then keep them as a single species aquarium.

Single species tanks can look just as attractive as mixed tanks, and many of the ideas in this book are designed with a particular fish in mind. Alternative fish are recommended for each design, but check with your aquarium store if you wish to substitute with other breeds.

Some breeds of fish are boisterous and when kept with similar types of fish, this can lead to shoals hunting down other fish. Red Snake Heads, Shark Catfish, and several breeds of Cichlid can also be very aggressive towards other species of fish, so always check with your

aquarium store before selecting for your tank. Take special care with Angelfish— they are beautiful to look at but can be boisterous and aggresive once they get beyond a certain size. In contrast, certain species of Cichlid, like young Blue and Brown Acaras, Keyhole Cichlids, Checkerboard Cichlids, and Kribensis, are normally peaceful and a better bet for a community tank for larger fish.

TIMID FISH

Guppies and Neon Tetras, Ruby Barbs, and Glowlight Tetras tend to be the whipping boys of aquarium life because of their small size and bright colors. They are prone to attack by Angelfish and other aggressive fish, so only keep these species with other small and peaceful fish. Neon Tetras are at special risk and will be viewed as live food by larger tank inhabitants. They also tend to need a more specified water quality than other fish, so this can affect their life span once inside the tank.

WATER QUALITY

When you select fish, always check the water quality they require, as this can affect their life span and breeding capabilities inside the tank.

Tetras, for example, prefer a soft, slightly acidic water that can be created with the use of special kits. Always follow the

manufacturer's instructions and ask at your aquarium store about the appropriate use of these products.

AQUARIUM FRIENDS

Fish are not the only creatures that can be kept in a tropical aquarium. Freshwater crabs are great fun and provide extra visual interest. With their distinctive red claws, Thai Crabs are particularly pretty and will scuttle about the tank floor happily picking at leftover fish food. However, it is important to note that crabs cannot survive on debris alone. Frozen worms can be bought from most aquarium stores and will provide much needed nutrients. If keeping crabs in your aquarium, it is wise to remember that they can be

avid gardeners and will pull up plants and move sand, and turn over rocks. Even though snails are often thought to be a handy way of keeping the tank walls clean and free from algae, snails are asexual and don't need two sexes to produce offspring. Therefore, a single snail in your tank will rapidly multiply to a thousand snails and eat all your plants.

Aquarium frogs can also be an interesting addition to your tank. Being so lively, a tank with several frogs will always have something interesting going on. Unlike normal frogs, these aquarium frogs don't

need to spend time on dry land and can live their whole lives in the water. It is best to keep frogs with peaceful fish, since their legs can be nipped by aggressive fish.

PLANTS

Correct positioning of the selected plant life is essential for a successful aquarium design. Careful placement of plants will avoid the situation where larger plants obscure both the fish and other plants. Plants such as Cabomba, Myriophyllum, and Straight Vallis are all best kept at the back of the tank. Although there is slightly less light at the back of the tank, these plants will still grow to a decent size and provide an attractive background, showing off your fish well and providing welcome shelter for smaller fish.

Keep smaller plants such as Lobelia, Pygmy Chain Sword Plants, and Fountain Plants to the front of the tank. Also be aware of which fish you're planning to put in your tank when selecting plants, as some fish, such as several species of Cichlid, will pull up plants or tear off leaves. In these cases, it might be best to choose a design with mainly rocks, woods, or artificial plants. Many of the artificial plants on the market are as effective as the real thing and can greatly help to fill a tank with greenery. They will also free you from the constant maintenance required by genuine plant life.

basic DESIGN RULES

Your tank is not only a home for your fish, it is your very own work of art. Follow a series of basic design rules to ensure that your fish feel comfortable in their environment and give your own living space the exciting, unique feel that only an aquarium can provide.

GENERAL CONSIDERATIONS

For a well-designed tank, you need to consider several points. First, you must design a tank in which your fish will feel at ease. Make sure there is enough shade, free water space, and that the fish are safe with their co-inhabitants. Always try to look at it from the perspective of the fish and consider their needs first.

Second, treat the empty tank as a blank canvas, and think about how you want to paint your "picture." The tank can be biospheric, constructed to mimic the natural habitat of the fish, with all the plants and materials coming from the same part of the world. Alternatively, it could be inspired by a natural environment you have experienced or imagined yourself, with a careful selection of plants, rocks, and wood. If you are feeling truly contemporary, you may wish to abandon traditional scenery altogether and use purely modern materials, such as glass pebbles.

THEMES

Before you start putting together your tank, you need to decide what the theme of your aquarium will be. The designs in this book will help you make up your mind. Unless you want a completely biospheric tank, you can mix some of the ideas from one design and put them with another, as long as it does not create any problems for your fish. Whatever you do with the designs, make sure that you choose suitable fish that are happy to live together.

NATURAL HABITATS

A tank that is designed with a natural habitat in mind is called a biospheric tank. These tanks use fish, plants, rocks, wood, and base materials from one specific geographic region and attempt to make the tank as natural as possible. Biospheric tanks are an ideal way of re-creating your favorite place in the world within the comfort of your very own home. The advantage of these tanks is that, very often, fish from the same regions have many of the same requirements and will be more compatible tank mates.

INSPIRED BY NATURE

Aquariums that involve a traditional combination of natural materials are a popular option for many fishkeepers. These tanks offer more flexibility than biospheric designs, since it is possible to introduce original materials, such as fossils or crystals, but still retain a link with the natural world.

Tank designs that retain a link with nature are soothing and peaceful environments that are pleasing to the eye and a joy to watch. However, it is vital to ensure that the fish are happy living alongside each other and that their water quality requirements are the same.

Let your imagination run wild!

FUN AND FUNKY

If you are feeling adventurous and wish to introduce a sense of fun into your aquarium, why not opt for a contemporary design. Man-made products, such as plastic, polymer clay, glass pebbles, and synthetic plants can be employed in a creative, tasteful, and magical way to create new and exciting tank environments, transformed to look natural and exciting in the aquarium.

Even everyday objects such as stainless steel kitchen utensils and glass lamp shades can be used in your aquarium. As long as your selected materials are properly prepared and treated to protect the fish, you can really let your imagination run wild. Of course, the great thing about modern tank designs is that they are easy to change around, so if you get bored with your design you can transform the tank with a completely new look.

Plant-free tanks will result in a reduced amount of shade for the fish. It is vital that you turn off the aquarium light for as long as possible so that the fish may rest. Check with your aquarium store that your chosen fish are suitable for your chosen design.

Rocks make ideal focal points. Dappled rocks appear rougher than those with a smooth texture.

Use similarly colored plants and rocks to create a unified theme.

LAYOUT

Decide whether you want a formal or informal layout for your aquarium. A formal design will be quite structured with more traditional fish, plants, and ornaments, whereas an informal design will be more free flowing with, for example, more plants, wood, or variations on any of the themes in this book. Make sure that whichever design you choose, the objects you add to your tank are safe for your fish.

FOCAL POINTS

To create the most effective designs, ensure that your tank has a focal point. Creating an effective focal point is a way of planting or placing an object so that it draws your eye to a certain part of the aquarium. If you have a particularly interesting rock or piece of wood, try placing it just off-center in your tank, and then plant a few pale plants behind it to help make it stand out more. Alternatively, you could place a large piece of rock or coal near the back, then plant low-growing plants or smaller rocks near the front to create a feeling of depth. This will give a strong focal point in your tank, leaving you free to add smaller features to the other parts of the aquarium.

When designing your tank remember the motto "less is more:" the fewer items you have in your tank, the better it will look. Over-filling the tank will make it cluttered.

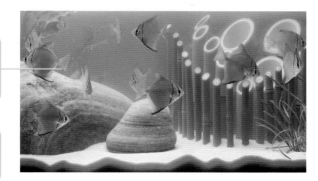

Decide whether you want a formal layout ...

... or an informal one

Create a strong focal point

Less is more

Harmonize your colors so that they work well together

TEXTURES

Your choice of scenery will naturally determine the textural feel of your tank. All the materials available to you have their own particular characteristics, and these can be exploited to great effect.

Consider the basic qualities of the most commonly used materials. Sand is much finer than gravel and can be used to create soft swirls and patterns on the base layer. However, gravel provides greater interest in terms of color and is ideal for simulating a natural riverbed.

Man-made glass pebbles have a formal uniform shape suitable for a modern aquarium design, whereas tumbled glass chippings create a more random texture.

Each piece of rock and wood is totally unique in terms of shape, texture, and pattern. The underside of a piece of wood will reveal the roughness of the root system, whereas the top side will be much smoother, since it lies under the bark.

Rough and smooth, mix your textures

COLORS

Before purchasing any fish, plants, or scenery, decide on the colors you want to use in your tank design. If you prefer strong colors, you may like to select artificial plants and colored gravel. These may be combined with more muted background colors to help them stand out. If you are using natural products, you can still select items around a distinct color theme. Red, white, or yellow rocks create a completely different look than gray or black rocks.

Available in a host of different shades and sizes, manufactured glass pebbles and tumbled glass chipping provide a stunningly colorful base layer. They can also be scattered over a natural base layer, such as gravel, for a more subtle effect.

safety and
YOUR FISH

Your aquarium will be home for your fish. They are totally reliant on you to provide them with a safe, enjoyable, and comfortable place in which to live. Just as you would never let a child play on the highway, you cannot expect your fish to exist in an unsafe environment. It is your responsibility to make sure that there are no damaging chemicals, rough surfaces, or narrow spaces in which they may trap themselves. If you follow these guidelines, your aquarium will be a safe and happy place for your fish. Always check with your aquarium store before using any products that are not specifically designed for aquarium use.

STONES AND ROCKS

To make sure that stones and rocks have no sharp edges, rub them against each other or use wet-dry sandpaper. This will smooth down any chips or roughness that could rub the scales off your fish and leave them open to infection. Rinse well under running water to remove excess dust.

If you do not know exactly where your rocks have come from, then you need to make sure they are not harboring any dangerous chemicals or other pollutants. Prepare a bucket of clean water with a little bleach added to it. Soak the rocks in the solution for at least 1 day to kill off any bacteria or unsafe chemicals. After you have soaked the rocks, rinse them continuously in clean water until the smell of bleach is totally removed. Scrub the rocks with a brush, then leave to soak overnight in a bucket of clean water. Change the water again, and then soak for another night. Take the time and trouble to do this properly, as any detergents, chemicals, or cleaning products remaining on the rocks, stones, or other objects could pollute the aquarium water and kill the fish.

Some rocks and stones can alter the pH balance of water, make sure they are suitable before use. Never use rocks of an alkaline nature, such as limestone or sandstone. Always stick to hard rocks, such as igneous granite. To check the suitability of rock, pour some vinegar onto the surface. If it runs off easily, then the rock is safe. If, however, the vinegar starts to fizz on the surface, then it is reacting with the alkaline chemicals in the rock. This shows that the rock will dissolve in the water and affect the pH.

WOOD

Bogwood, or water-worn wood, sold by aquarium stores, is the most suitable wood to use in an aquarium. To make sure that the wood is free from dust, dirt, and pollutants, scrub it thoroughly under running water, then soak in clean water overnight. Change the water and soak again overnight. Never use driftwood from the beach, since it will contain pollutants. Bamboo and synthetic wood also make ideal additions to a tank.

SAND, PEBBLES, AND GRAVEL

Before using sand, pebbles, or gravel, make sure that they are thoroughly clean. The most effective cleaning method is to quarter-fill a bucket with the chosen material and rinse under running water while swirling the mixture around with your hand. When cleaning sand, be careful not to stir too vigorously, since it can easily spill out over the top of the bucket—simply swirl the water and lift the sand gently from the bottom of the bucket to rinse the grains. You will be surprised at the amount of dirt that comes out when you drain off the water. Drain off the water by keeping your hand over the sand and leaning the bucket to one side so that the dirty water can run away. Drain as much as you can without the sand escaping past your hand. Rinse out several times until the water runs clear. Colored gravel needs extra soaking to remove the dye.

Chicken wire must be carefully sealed to prevent rusting.

Smooth glass beads are safe and pretty.

Make sure your paint is non-toxic and waterproof.

GLASS

Some of the designs in this book use glass pebbles or tumbled glass chippings as a base layer. Tumbled glass chippings are available from glass manufacturers and are often used as garden scenery. The chippings have been machine-tumbled to smooth off the sharp edges. Do not use regular glass chippings, since these will cut the fish if they swim against them. Smooth and oval in shape, glass pebbles are stocked by craft suppliers and specialty manufacturers. They are available in a range of colors, shapes, and sizes.

METAL

Ideally, any metal used in a fish tank should be stainless steel so that it will not rust and poison the water. If you have to use a metal that is not stainless steel, however, it is essential that you coat it in acrylic or aquarium sealant or marine spar varnish to prevent corrosion.

Galvanized chicken wire is ideal for building tank scenery, but must be coated in acrylic sealant or marine spar vanish, or completely enclosed by another material, such as polymer clay, to act as a waterproof seal around the metal. Do not use any kind of alloy, aluminium, or tin metal in your tank.

PLASTIC

Plastic is safe to use in fish tanks, but must be checked for rough edges before use. Rough edges can be found on seams or edges of molded plastic, and must be smoothed with wet-dry sandpaper before use. In addition, all plastic ornaments and scenery must be thoroughly cleaned before use—scrub vigorously under running water, then soak overnight in clean water.

CERAMICS

It is best to select glazed items, since these have a sealed surface. Clean well before use. If using unglazed ceramics, clean in the same way as stones or rocks to ensure any pollutants are removed. If using ceramics with painted decoration, check that the paint is non-toxic, and also coat the item in acrylic sealant.

MODELER'S POLYSTYRENE

When using modeler's polystyrene to construct scenery, take care to select the dense, finely textured variety, rather than the polystyrene made of individual balls, since these will seriously harm your fish. If you need to stick blocks of polystyrene together, make sure to use aquarium silicone adhesive or PVA wood adhesive, as these will not pollute the water when dry. When positioning your scenery in the tank, make sure there is no space left between the tank and the polystyrene, since the fish could become trapped. Your fish may swim into small crevices when they are nervous and become trapped. Either leave plenty of space or make sure the scenery is flush to the tank glass.

MODELING MATERIALS

When making scenery, use only non-toxic modeling materials, such as polymer clay. Always request a detailed breakdown of ingredients from the manufacturer and check with your aquarium store that they are safe for your fish. Do not use regular clay as this will leak toxins.

• CLEANLINESS •
Everything in your tank must be spotlessly clean before fish and water are added. If using detergents to clean the tank or scenery, rinse thoroughly to remove any residue.

• ADHESIVES AND GLUE •
Always use aquarium silicone adhesive to position props and scenery in your tank, since it is specially designed for building aquariums and will not pollute the water. This adhesive must be left to harden for at least 2 days before water is added to the tank. Ask at your aquarium store for details of this product. PVA wood can also be used to make scenery, but always ask the manufacturers for a detailed breakdown of ingredients and check with your aquarium store that these are safe.

• PAINT •
If you are painting your tank scenery, make sure that you use a non-toxic, waterproof, acrylic paint. Swimming pool paint is also suitable. Ask the manufacturer for a breakdown of ingredients, and check with your aquarium store that the paint is safe to use. When you are painting any object, make sure you apply the coats evenly and thinly before allowing it to dry for at least 2 days. Ask at your aquatic center for further advice if you are unsure.

• VARNISH •
Marine spar, or yacht varnish is the most suitable varnish for use in your tank, since it is clear and water-resistant. Be aware that even waterproof varnish may begin to peel or lift after a few weeks underwater, so you may have to remove scenery and check for deterioration.

• ADHESIVE PUTTY •
Do not under any circumstances use adhesive putty to secure props in your fish tank. It contains dangerous chemicals that will pollute your water.

the DESIGNS

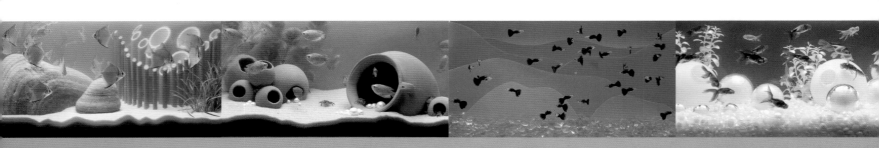

malaysian
STREAM

With all the elegance of Southeast Asia, this aquarium is peaceful, natural, and the image of a gently flowing Malaysian stream.

An informed mixture of sand, gravel, and pebbles makes this simulated Asian riverbed totally convincing. An inspirationally green aquarium, it is populated by fast-moving Barbs and Red-Finned Sharks.

THE CAST

TIGER BARB
Tiger Barbs are very agile, and always make exciting viewing. Being such confident fish means that they will provide a fascinating display towards the front of the tank. They will form a shoal and dart in between each other and the plants. Use 10 to 15 fish in this tank.

GREEN TIGER BARB
Green Tiger Barbs have identical behavior patterns to their striped cousins, but they have beautiful, bottle-green markings on the body, which are set off by red and black fins, and a silver underbelly. Use 10 to 15 fish in a medium-sized tank.

RED-FINNED SHARK
Bottom-feeders, Red-Finned Sharks are colorful additions to the tank. They have elongated black bodies and bright red fins. Hardy fish from the Cyprinidae family, they can live for several years in a well-maintained aquarium. Use 1 or 2 fish, depending on tank size.

• FISH CARE •
Red-Finned Sharks are territorial. They are best kept alone, since 2 or more can fight each other and become aggressive. If the tank is large enough, then 2 or more may be kept, because they will then define their own living space.

THE SCENERY

▼ ❶ SILICA SAND
For the base layer of the tank, use around 45lb (20kg) sand.

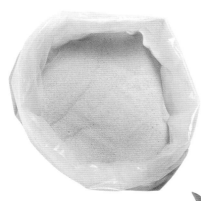

▲ ❹ FINE PEA GRAVEL
For a subtle covering, you'll need just a couple of handfuls of fine bore pea gravel to scatter over the sand.

▶ ❺ RED ROCKS
Select 2 or 3 red rocks, measuring approximately one-sixth the length of the tank. Take care to select non-alkaline rocks, such as volcanic rhyolite or red granite. Synthetic aquarium rocks are also ideal.

◀ ❷ PEBBLES
Use about 8 pebbles with pink and gray tones. Each one should be approximately one-tenth the length of the tank.

▶ ❻ FOUNTAIN PLANT
Fountain Plants are indigenous to Southeast Asia and add interest to the front of the tank. You will need 5 to 6 similarly sized Fountain Plants for this tank.

▶ ❸ GIANT INDIAN WATER STAR
Giant Indian Water Star, a large, broad leafed plant, will provide interest, creating both a natural backdrop and a useful hiding place for your fish. Use about 8 plants, depending on size.

STAGE SET-UP
Lay the sand as the base layer, and scatter the gravel over the sand near the front. Arrange the pebbles mainly to the right and side along the center, and the red rocks to the left. Position the Giant Indian Water Stars along the back of the tank, leaving a gap just off center. Position the fountain plants in front of the Giant Indian Water Stars, spaced between the pebbles and rocks.

ALTERNATIVE FISH

ZEBRA DANIO
The active Zebra Danio provides plenty of visual interest, as they love to dart around the tank in groups. The black and silver stripes on its body help it to stand out in the tank, and as the fish turns in the light, you will catch sight of a green hue to the scales. Use as an alternative or addition to the tank, adjusting the total number of fish accordingly.

BLACK RUBY BARB
The brightly colored Black Ruby Barb is a welcome addition to any tank. It has a Goldfish-like body, but is much more colorful. The male turns a very bright red, whereas the female is slightly more silvery when in peak breeding condition. Use with any of the other fish suggested for this tank.

ADD TO THE LOOK

Add color to this tank by mixing in some Red Cabomba plants alongside the green plants. You could also use Water Milfoil and Hairgrass.

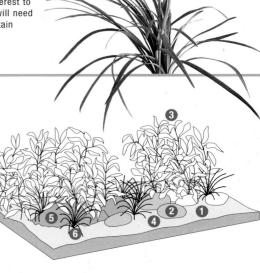

thai
BEACH

Reminiscent of the shores of a castaway island, this luscious aquarium creates the exotic atmosphere of Southeast Asia, giving you a hint of warm tropical waters.

Using beautiful plants and animals indigenous to Thailand and the surrounding coastline, this tank is easy to maintain as it only requires a low water level. With more interest than your usual vacation resort beach, your Thai beach aquarium gives the wistful adventurer in you warmer climes to dream of.

THE CAST

RED-CLAWED THAI CRAB

The small and attractive Red-Clawed Thai Crab provides plenty of amusement, interest, and enjoyment. Always on the move, these crabs enjoy climbing. They are also a great asset as they clean away any scraps of leftover food in the tank. Use up to 10 crabs for a medium-sized tank.

SPARKLING GOURAMI

Sparkling Gouramis are small and active fish from Southeast Asia. They look completely different from their Gourami cousins because of the environment they are naturally found in. As they thrive in shallow waters and rock pools, these are the perfect fish for this tank. For the best display use 20 fish for a medium-sized tank.

• FISH CARE •

Thai crabs really enjoy climbing, so ensure that there is no way of them escaping if they happen to climb up the air pipe or thermometer. As crabs can be quite territorial, it is wise to introduce all the crustaceans at the same time, and make sure they are all of equal size to avoid fights. Be aware that crabs are avid gardeners and will probably try to rearrange your plant display!

THE SCENERY

◀ ❶ YELLOW AQUARIUM ROCKS

Use 3 to 4 pieces of sand-colored aquarium rock to build up the beach area. Each piece should be no longer than one-fifth the length of the tank. Choose rocks with holes to create pools and caves for the fish to hide in.

• ROCK CARE •

Before filling your tank, check the rocks for sharp edges and sand them down. Wash the rocks well to remove any dust. Refer to pages 12–13 for more information on preparing your tank scenery.

STAGE SET-UP

Position the wood and rocks along the center of the tank to create a wall effect one-third the height of the tank. (This is the intended level of the finished beach.) Place gravel behind the rocks and wood to fix them in position and create a base for the beach. Slope the gravel up towards the back of the tank. Carefully pour the sand over the gravel, wood, and rocks to fill any gaps and create a slope. Allow the sand to flow down over the rocks towards the front of the tank, keeping a depression towards the center-front area. Plant the Dracena on each side, and the Arrowhead around the Dracena on the right. Scatter small shells over the sand at the back to complete the beach. Slowly add the water to the height of the wall, then gently scoop the water over the beach to smooth the sandy slope.

▶ ❷ MOPANI BOGWOOD

Mopani bogwood is harder and paler than ordinary bogwood. Select 2 pieces of wood to place in the water and on the beach. Each piece of wood should be about one-third the length of the tank.

◀ ❸ GREEN DRACENA

These tall and waxy leafed plants are perfect for creating that tropical beach look. Use 4 plants.

◀ ❹ ARROWHEAD

An attractive plant, Arrowhead has three pronged leaves and thrives in this type of environment. Use 2 to 3 plants.

▲ ❺ SHELLS

Use a selection of small, attractive sea shells such as mini cowries and conches to help create that beach-like feeling in the tank. Scatter them randomly above the waterline. Use 20 to 25 shells.

▶ ❻ YELLOW GRAVEL

Use plenty of sand-colored gravel to build up the base layer behind the rocks, secure the beach structure, and prevent the sand flowing into the water. Wash the gravel well before use. For a medium-sized tank, use 33lb (15kg) gravel.

▶ ❼ SILICA SAND

Use silica sand to completely cover the gravel base layer. For a medium-sized tank, you will need about 45lb (20kg) sand. Take care when adding the sand to the tank, since it can easily stick to the sides, and be careful when adding the water, otherwise the sandy slope may slip down into the water.

ALTERNATIVE FISH

CHERRY BARB

The small and colorful red Cherry Barb comes from Southeast Asia Use up to 20 fish for a medium-sized tank.

ADD TO THE LOOK

You could change the aspect of this tank by adding more rocks or plants, building the beach higher, or by using different plant varieties. If you choose to build your beach to a higher level and therefore have more water in the tank, make sure the plants you choose still fit properly inside your beach aquarium and don't peek out over the edge of your tank!

east african
ROCKY LAKE

A rough-and-ready, biospheric aquarium, this tank is easy to maintain, and provides many hideouts from where your fish can observe you watching them.

Modeled on the bottom of a Central or East African rocky lake, this tank is a myriad of shapes and colors with the hard surfaces of rocks, boulders, and pebbles creating a sharp contrast to the sleek elegance of the fish. With effective planning, ledges and bridges can be created to provide shelter where your fish will feel safe and comfortable. A bare and simple design makes this low-maintenance aquarium ideal for someone with a busy lifestyle and minimalist tastes.

THE CAST

FRONTOSA
The striking, dark gray striped markings of Frontosa look very showy against the pebbles and rocks. Simple but effective, between 10 and 15 of these Cichlids create a fantastic show in front of the hard rocks. The fish will reward you with hours of pleasure as you watch them dart between the rocks and hide from each other in the crevices.

ALTERNATIVE FISH

RED EYE TETRA
These large, silver Tetras have bright red eyes and a black stripe by the base of the tail. Choose them instead of Frontosa, either on their own or combined with Angelfish and Scissortails.

ANGELFISH
Large Cichlids with elongated fins and silver, white, and black coloring, Angelfish are elegant alternatives to Frontosa in this type of aquarium. However, they can be aggressive to smaller or long-finned species, so only select small ones, which may be grouped with Tetras and Scissortails.

THE SCENERY

▶ ❶ ROUND BOULDERS

Use 2 or 3 three large boulders of igneous rock, such as granite, to create a feeling of strength and permanence. The shape of the boulders also complements the surrounding pebbles, giving the sense that this underwater landscape has simply tumbled into place. Make sure they are no larger than one-quarter of the length of the tank.

• ROCK CARE •

To protect the fish, rub together the edges of the boulders and rocks before use to smooth any rough edges. Refer to pages 12–13 for more information on fish safety and preparing your aquarium scenery.

◀ ❷ FLAT ROCKS

Use 2 to 3 slabs of hard flat rock, such as slate or schist, to support the pebbles and boulders, and build up the overhanging crevices, where your fish can hide. These should be no longer than one-fifth the length of the tank. Smooth edges before use.

▶ ❹ PEBBLES

Create the bulk of the living space with smooth pebbles. You'll need about 20 pebbles for a medium-sized tank, and they should be 3 in to 6 in (7.5cm to 15cm) in diameter. As each pebble is unique in shape, size, and color, together they provide plenty of visual interest in this plant-free tank.

▶ ❸ PEA GRAVEL

Smoother than regular gravel, pea gravel is widely available from aquatic centers in a choice of 2 sizes. It provides a good base and helps to anchor the rocks in an upright position. Its mixed shading matches the color of the rocks and pebbles. For a 3 in (7.5cm) layer in a medium tank, you will need about 33lb (15kg).

STAGE SET-UP

Lay the gravel, bringing it up the sides of the tank to create a slight dip in the center. Place the boulders on either side of the central dip, pressing them firmly in the gravel. Create the "roof" of the main cavern with a large piece of flat rock, then carefully place the large pebbles on top. Take care to position the pebbles securely, gluing them into place with aquarium silicone adhesive if necessary. Create as many crevices as possible where the fish can rest.

ADD TO THE LOOK

SCISSORTAIL

Scissortails have long silver bodies and exaggerated caudal fins that sport a large black dot at the end of each lobe. The name comes from the distinctive twitching motion of the caudal fin. A good alternative to Frontosa, Scissortails also work well with Tetras and Angelfish.

• FISH CARE •

As there are no plants to provide shelter, it is important that the fish have enough hiding places between the rocks. Because the pebbles and rocks are mostly rounded, the spaces where they touch create little gaps suitable for the fish, so build up as many pebbles as you can against the back of the tank. Use the gravel to help anchor the pebbles, boulders, and rocks in place at the rear of the aquarium.

To break away from the silver theme, you may wish to introduce yellow Cichlids to stand out dramatically against the gray pebbles. Other alternatives are Ruby or Rosy Barbs, Dwarf Gouramis or Swordtails.

amazon
BASIN

A peaceful and relaxing atmosphere emanates from this aquarium. On a South American theme, this tank is just like the bottom of a clear, freshwater lake in the Amazon Basin.

Using fish and plants that are indigenous to the area around the Amazon, you can create your very own part of the tropical rain forest. This tank design is constructed to replicate conditions occurring in the wild, using a range colorful tetras.

THE CAST

CARDINAL TETRA
Bold and brightly colored, Cardinal Tetras shoal in superb style when kept in large groups. Use 15 to 20 for this tank.

GLOWLIGHT TETRA
Similar to the Cardinals, Glowlight Tetras are brightly colored and also shoal spectacularly when kept in groups. Use 15 to 20 in this tank.

LEMON TETRA
Although Lemon Tetras are not as colorful as their relatives, they are from the same region of South America and have a very dramatic body shape.

ALTERNATIVE FISH

SILVER-TIPPED TETRA
Even though they are not as colorful as other Tetra relatives, Silver-Tipped Tetras are a strong addition to any tank. They are brown with white flecks on the tips of their fins and their tail.

THE SCENERY

▶ ❶ BOGWOOD
Select 3 or 4 interesting pieces of bogwood to provide the defining structure of the aquarium. Each piece should be between one-quarter and one-third the size of the tank.

▶ ❷ PEA GRAVEL
For a good, uniform layer, use 33lbs (15kg) of gravel in a medium-sized tank. This will be sufficient for a good 3 in (7.5cm) layer.

◀ ❸ GREEN CABOMBA
Use 4 to 5 Green Cabomba plants at the rear of the tank. They add a wonderful bushy feel to the environment.

▶ ❹ PYGMY CHAIN SWORD PLANT
Another variation of the Sword Plant, this variety is also ideal for filling small foreground gaps. Use 1 plant.

STAGE SET-UP
First, lay down your gravel for the base. Arrange the wood along the center of the tank, keeping the taller parts toward the sides to create a low point just off-center. Plant the Cabomba along the back of the bogwood, leaving a gap in the center for the larger Dwarf Amazon Sword Plants. Plant the smaller Dwarf Amazon and Pygmy Chain Sword Plants on the right-hand side, in front of the wood. Finally, plant 2 small clumps of Hairgrass in the gaps between the wood left of the Pigmy Chain Sword Plant.

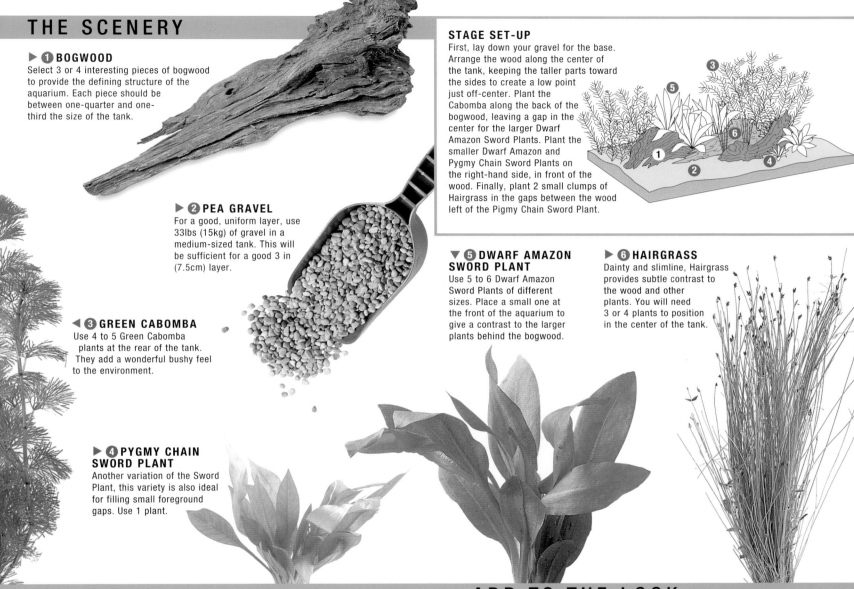

▼ ❺ DWARF AMAZON SWORD PLANT
Use 5 to 6 Dwarf Amazon Sword Plants of different sizes. Place a small one at the front of the aquarium to give a contrast to the larger plants behind the bogwood.

▶ ❻ HAIRGRASS
Dainty and slimline, Hairgrass provides subtle contrast to the wood and other plants. You will need 3 or 4 plants to position in the center of the tank.

ADD TO THE LOOK

HEAD-AND-TAIL-LIGHT TETRA
These attractive, slim fish are also known as Beacon Fish, because of the glowing dots by their eyes and by the base of their tails. Apart from these dots they are virtually transparent.

• FISH CARE •
Make sure that the water is of the right quality for Tetras. Ask at your aquarium store for details. The Cardinal Tetra may lose some color when first transferred into the main tank, but with a few hours of peace and quiet, will soon return to the full concentration of color.

Add contrast to this tank by mixing in some Red Cabomba for extra color alongside the Green Cabomba. You could also use Water Milfoil and Hairgrass, both of which are from the same region in the Amazon Basin.

central american coastal
STREAM

Rough, gritty, and full of life, this busy natural habitat echoes the home environment of some of our most popular aquarium fish.

Mollies, Swordtails, and Guppies all come from this part of the world, and you can now have fun re-creating a home away from home for them as you assemble this tank. You will be able to enjoy your fish in the knowledge that they are thriving in the closest re-creation of their natural home that you can provide. Because the fish feel they are in their natural surroundings, you will notice that they are more relaxed and behave more instinctively—especially when it comes to breeding!

THE CAST

GUPPY
A mix of colorful and enjoyable Guppies will add a graceful, yet lively atmosphere to your tank. Use 15 to 20 fish.

GREEN SWORDTAIL
The Green Swordtail, slightly duller than the more common Red Swordtail, is found naturally in Central American streams. Use about 10 fish.

BLACK MOLLY
A live-breeder, the Black Molly stands out strikingly against the colors and shapes of the other fish. Use 2 to 3 fish for a medium-sized tank.

• FISH CARE •
Guppies, Swordtails, and Mollies are all live-breeders, so do not be surprised if a few live fry appear after a few weeks.

THE SCENERY

▶ ❶ SILICA SAND
Mixing in a handful of aquarium sand with the top layer of gravel helps to create the illusion of coastal waters bringing in sand from the ocean.

◀ ❺ PEA GRAVEL
Use standard aquarium gravel for an authentic base layer. For a 3 in (7.5cm) layer in a medium-sized aquarium, you will need about 33lb (15kg).

▶ ❼ TWISTED VALLIS
Creating height and interest at the rear of the tank, the Twisted Vallis is perfect for a biospheric tank from this region. Use up to 10 plants for a really lush finish.

▶ ❷ PEBBLES
Select 1 or 2 large pebbles for the corner of the tank to help create the coastal element. The pebbles should be no larger than one-eighth the length of the tank.

▶ ❻ GREEN CABOMBA
The attractive and bushy Green Cabomba plant is typical of those found in the Central American region. Use 3 plants for this tank.

◀ ❸ BOGWOOD
Use 3 pieces of bogwood of various sizes and shapes. Synthetic aquarium wood can also be used, since it gives an extremely realistic effect.

▶ ❹ FLAT STONES
Select about 25 small, flat stones or pebbles to enhance the natural look of this tank. Look out for green-tinted stones as a change from the usual brown or beige color.

STAGE SET-UP
Lay the gravel on the floor of the tank and sprinkle the surface with half of the sand. Arrange 3 pieces of wood along the length of the tank, keeping the taller pieces to the sides. Plant the Twisted Vallis behind the wood in each corner of the tank, then plant the Green Cabomba slightly off-center. Place the pebbles and stones at the front of the tank. Sprinkle the remaining sand over the stones and wood.

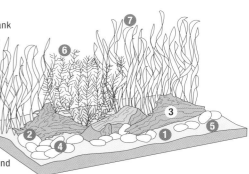

ALTERNATIVE FISH

RED SWORDTAIL
Brighter and more exotic-looking than its green cousin, the Red Swordtail looks good in any tank.

BLUE ACARA
A large and peaceful fish, the Blue Acara is good in any community tank that does not house very small fish. These gray fish have vertical bands and turquoise dots, as well as stunning blue markings on the face and side of the head.

PLATY
From the same geographical area as Guppies, Mollies, and Swordtails, Platies are equally lively and fun to keep.

ADD TO THE LOOK

You could add to the appearance by scattering a few cleaned shells over the floor of the tank. Alternatively, increase the amount of sand to create the effect that the fish are closer to the ocean.

lush
PARADISE

An organic yet luxuriant-looking aquarium, the lush paradise tank may seem intricate, but is simple to set up. It provides a tranquil and rich-looking habitat for your fish. They will feel safe and secure in the shelter of this ever-moving green environment.

To get the most from this aquarium, use as wide a selection of aquatic plants as possible, then fill with the most brightly colored and active fish that will live happily together in a community tank. This traditional design will provide the fish enthusiast with a calming and verdant aquarium that brings a miniature tropical lagoon right into the suburban home.

THE CAST

TIGER BARB
Tiger Barbs are active and confident fish, and make a lively and colorful addition to your tank. They can irritate other fish, nipping at those with long fins, but in small groups of 5 to 10, they will add excitement and perk up an otherwise docile tank. Use 10 fish for a medium-sized tank.

GOLD COMET SWORDTAIL
The yellow and gold color of the active Gold Comet Swordtails is particularly distinctive against the greenery of this plant-based tank. Use 10 fish for a medium-sized tank.

RAM
Attractive and less aggressive than some other species of Cichlid, the Ram is a good fish in a community tank. Keep in groups of 8 or more to add character and color. Use 10 fish for a medium-sized tank.

ALTERNATIVE FISH

GUPPY
Graceful and serene, the male Guppies will float elegantly around the plants, whereas the females will busily dart just above them, or nestle in the shelter of the leaves. Use around 10 in a medium-sized tank, with a ratio of 4 females to every male.

THE SCENERY

◀ **1** FINE PEA GRAVEL
Use smaller bore pea gravel, measuring about ¼ in (6mm) in diameter, to anchor the plants in this tank. For a 3 in (7.5cm) layer in a medium-sized tank, use about 33lb (15kg).

◀ **2** CRYPTOCORYNE BLASSII

This broad-leaved Cryptocoryne adds a green focal point to the foliage in the front of the tank. Use 1 plant.

▶ **3** FOUNTAIN PLANT
Spiky and grass-like, this plant shape contrasts effectively positioned at the front of the tank. Use about 5 plants.

◀ **4** DWARF AMAZON SWORD PLANT
With its broad, smooth leaves, Sword Plants are used in this tank and contrast well with the other plants. Use 3 to 4 plants.

◀ **5** TWISTED VALLIS
The long, twisted leaves of this plant add height and interest to the tank. Use 2 to 3 plants, depending on size.

◀ **6** RED LOBELIA

A small plant useful for filling out the front of the tank. Use 9 plants.

▲ **7** INDIAN FERN
This fast-growing plant varies in color according to lighting conditions. Use 2 to 3 plants.

▲ **8** RED LUDWIGIA
Broad, red leaves add bold color. Use 2 plants.

▼ **9** SPATHIPHYLLUM WALLISII
The imposing Spathiphyllum Wallisii is similar to the Amazon Sword Plant, but is distinguished by a gently undulating leaf edge. Use 3 to 4 plants.

◀ **10** BABY TEARS
This small-leaved plant is ideal for filling gaps. Use 2 to 3 plants.

▶ **11** MYRIOPHYLLUM

Similar to Cabomba, but bushier, this plant will fill out the gaps in your tank. Use 2 to 3 plants. For a more slender look, try replacing with Mayaca Fluviatillis.

◀ **12** UMBRELLA FERN
With broad leaves and tall stems, the Umbrella Fern adds plenty of shade and shelter for the fish. Use 2 to 3 plants.

▶ **13** GREEN CABOMBA
Green Cabomba is a popular spawning medium and will root easily in the tank. Use 1 to 2 plants, depending on size. Remove any stems if the tank sediment causes them to clog.

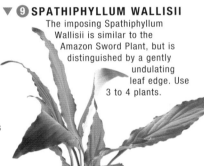

HONEY GOURAMI
The Honey Gourami will peacefully coexist in a community tank. It changes colors when threatened or if putting on a mating display. These Gouramis are happiest when kept in male-female pairs. Use 4 pairs of fish for a medium-sized tank.

HARALD SHULTZ'S CORY
To keep the bottom of this tank clean, it would be a good idea to have a couple of these small catfish in your aquarium.

STAGE SET-UP
Lay the gravel base. Position the taller and bushier plants, such as the Umbrella Fern, Twisted Vallis, Green Cabomba, and Myriophyllum at the back. Plant the medium-sized Spathiphyllum Wallisii, Baby Tears, Dwarf Amazon Sword Plant, and Indian Fern in the middle of the tank, mixing the leaf shapes and adding in a dash of red with the Red Ludwigia. Graduate the plant size toward the front finishing off with Fountain Plants around a row of Red Lobelia, broken by the single Cryptocoryne Blassii.

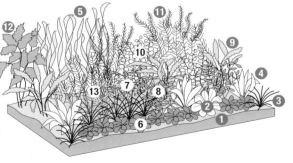

sheltered
HAVEN

Peaceful and serene, the sheltered haven is a more traditional type of aquarium. Using an uncomplicated design, you can create a habitat that makes a naturalistic showcase for brightly colored Tetras. You will be able to relax as you watch your fish dart between the plants and wood.

The natural wood and plants of the sheltered haven aquarium lend themselves perfectly to a tank best suited to shoals of fish that would congregate in the wild. Imagine a tropical lake, where years of uninterrupted breeding has led to millions of tiny fish living in a harmonious and colorful world—you can re-create this idyllic scene in your own home.

THE CAST

CARDINAL TETRA
Tiny but exciting in both color and movement, Cardinal Tetras have long been a true favorite of tropical aquarium keepers. They will create a dazzling display in your tank. The red and blue stripes that run along the body catch the light dramatically as the fish swoop and dive across your tank grouped in a massive shoal. Use about 150 fish for a medium-sized tank.

ALTERNATIVE FISH

NEON TETRA
Relatives of the Cardinal Tetra, Neon Tetras are very similar and provide much the same effect. They are somewhat smaller, with a slightly silvery sheen to the body, which makes them look a little paler. For the most effective display in a medium-sized tank, you'll need to use around 150 Neon Tetras.

GLOWLIGHT TETRA
The popular Glowlight Tetra has a silver body with a bright, almost luminous orange stripe running down the middle. When the fish are in prime condition the tips of their fins are white. Similar in habit to Neon Tetras, these fish enjoy moving around in large shoals, and will start shoaling when 10 or more are kept. Use about 100 fish for a medium-sized tank.

THE SCENERY

◀ ❶ FINE PEA GRAVEL
Use smaller bore pea gravel for this tank. Wash it well before use to remove any dust and impurities. For a 3 in (7.5cm) layer in a medium-sized tank, you'll need about 33lb (15kg).

❸ TWISTED VALLIS
This plant introduces feathery height to the tank. It also provides wavy fronds for your fish to swim through or hide behind. Use 2 groups of Twisted Vallis.

▼ ❺ FOUNTAIN PLANT
A small, spiky plant that looks effective positioned against the solid bulk of the wood and provides an angular shape in contrast to the more feathery Giant Twisted Vallis. Use 3 to 4 plants, depending on size.

▼ ❹ RED LOBELIA
Use a dwarf species of Red Lobelia to place toward the front of the tank to provide a prominent focal point. Use 2 or 3 plants, depending on size.

▼ ❷ WOOD
Use 3 or 4 large pieces of well-seasoned wood, and place in an attractive combination toward the center of your tank.

STAGE SET-UP
Lay the pea gravel base. Place the wood in the tank, keeping the tallest part of each piece near the center of the tank. Position the Twisted Vallis at the back corners of the tank. Place 1 Fountain Plant just off-center, positioning it so that it looks as though it is growing out of a piece of wood. Place another Fountain Plant on each side of the tank, also next to the wood. Finally, plant the Lobelia just off-center to the right, at the very front of the tank.

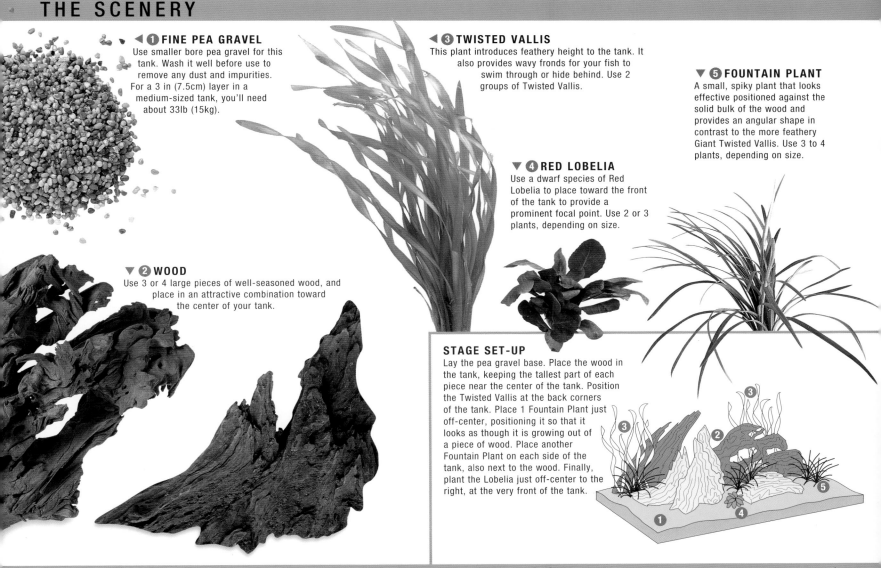

ADD TO THE LOOK

• FISH CARE •
When introducing new fish to an aquarium, it is wise to put them into quarantine for 2 days. Keeping a spare, smaller tank with an air pump as a dedicated quarantine tank is a sound investment, then when you buy any new fish you just pop them into it. Diseases such as white spot will show up in around a day and can be eradicated using a fish fungicide. Ask at your aquarium store for more information on using these products.

By combining different types of fish you'll get a subtly different look. Cardinal Tetras and Neon Tetras look equally as good when mixed with large numbers of Glowlight Tetras. Alter the plant varieties depending on the effect you want to achieve. Dwarf Anubias and Dwarf Amazon Sword Plants would give a lower, more rounded look. You could also change the wood for dark rocks, remembering to provide plenty of interesting crevices for these tiny fish to hide in.

Dwarf Amazon Sword Plant

Dward Anubias

meadow
SWEET

With a tranquil and serene air, this tank re-creates a country meadow on a hot summer's day, and provides a relaxing aquatic home for your fish.

This aquarium uses grasses and small aquatic plants to suggest a thriving country meadow, while bogwood creates the natural impression of a fallen log that is swarming with interesting inhabitants. Delicate, sedate fish add to the calming mood. The distinctive outlines of Gouramis and Angelfish are highlighted by the low-level plants and stunning blue backdrop behind the tank. Synthetic plants add to the lushness of the tank, without reducing the feeling of authenticity.

THE CAST

PEARL GOURAMI
With their dramatic mother-of-pearl dot markings and peaceful nature, Pearl Gouramis are perfect in this tank. Graceful and elegant, they are large enough not to be bullied by the Angelfish. For the best markings choose older, larger fish, as the younger fish are much paler. Colors are also intensified during breeding. Use no more than 6 in a medium-sized tank.

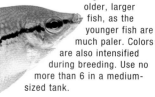

BLACK ANGELFISH
With their long fins, Black Angelfish will sit gracefully in the water and look both elegant and peaceful. Use 6 to 8 fish in a medium-sized tank.

ALTERNATIVE FISH

CONGO TETRA
From Zaire, the large and graceful Congo Tetra will float across your tank and weave in between the grasses in the backdrop. The Tetra's elongated fins show up well against bogwood. Use in place of the Gouramis and Marble Angelfish.

THE SCENERY

◀ ❶ PLASTIC FERN
To help increase the density of the planted area, use a tray of plastic aquarium fern. Select 2 different types of fern mats measuring approximately 4 in (10cm) square, with 2 in (5cm) fern sprouts. Use a different type of fern in each corner of the tank.

▲ ❺ PEA GRAVEL
For a medium-sized tank, use about 33lb (15kg) of gravel.

▶ ❼ HAIRGRASS
Hairgrass is the plant that truly creates a meadow-like feeling in this tank. Use a selection of both longer and shorter plants around the tank to create a wild look. Use about 3 plants.

▼ ❽ FOUNTAIN PLANT
The sharp and grass-like Fountain Plant creates the impression of a variety of grass species. Use around 6 Fountain Plants for a medium-sized tank.

▼ ❷ RED LOBELIA
Use 4–5 Red Lobelia to add variety to the plant-life. With their bright red tinge, you will create a contrast of colors too.

▼ ❻ PYGMY CHAIN SWORD PLANT
The flat leaves of the Pygmy Chain Sword Plant contrast well with the grass-like effect of the other plants. Use 6 of these plants in a medium-sized tank.

◀ ❸ BOGWOOD
Use 3 large pieces of bogwood to create the effect of fallen logs in the center of the "meadow."

▶ ❹ CRYPTOCORYNE BLASSII
Select a round-leaved variety of Cryptocoryne to position in the center-front area of the tank. You will need up to 3 plants, depending on size.

STAGE SET-UP
Lay the gravel base, taking care to make the front part slightly uneven. Stand 1 piece of wood in the center of the tank with 1 piece either side. Place the plastic ferns in the back corners, making sure that the base layer is buried out of sight. Position the real plants around the wood, using the smaller plants in the front and the larger plants at the back. Use some of the Hairgrass at the front to add height and interest.

ADD TO THE LOOK

CLOWN LOACH
With their orange-yellow and black stripes, bottom-dwelling Clown Loaches will busy themselves amongst the grasses rather like bumble bees working their way around the meadow looking for pollen. Use as alternatives, rather than additions to the fish used in this tank.

GUPPY
The bright colors of small Guppies will make them look like pretty butterflies hovering over a country meadow. Use as alternatives to the fish chosen for this tank.

• FISH CARE •
As there are many small plants in this tank, beware of feeding too much and too often, as any unwanted food will become lodged in the plants where the fish cannot reach it. This will pollute the water, making it harder for your fish to draw oxygen from it.

To increase the appearance of a grassy meadow, you could add extra Hairgrass and Fountain Plants, so that the whole base of the tank is filled with grassy plants.

sticks and
STONES

An aquarium full of contrasts, this tank is effective and visually exciting as well, providing variation and interest for both you and your fish.

Using twigs, smooth pebbles, and bogwood, this tank is a myriad of shapes and textures, creating an attractive backdrop which shows your fish off to powerful effect. This stimulating aquarium is also one in which your fish will feel safe and comfortable.

THE CAST

BLUE CORAL PLATY
Platies are robust and colorful, making a strong visual impact in any aquarium. As live-breeders, Platies are playful, and the males will chase the females in an intricate courtship dance. Plenty of live young can be brought to adulthood if kept in a breeding trap, until big enough to survive in the main tank.

ANGELICUS PIMELODELLA
You'll only need 1 or 2 of these lively catfish as they need quite a bit of room to dart about the tank. The soft pea gravel makes an ideal flooring, as they like to spend much of their time scavenging waste food. Replace with Pimelodella gracilis if unavailable.

• FISH CARE •
In order to create shade and shelter, carefully stack the pebbles on top of each other in small groups to create arches and gaps between them. Use the gravel to help anchor the pebbles in place. Position the bogwood at an angle to create shelter for the fish under its natural curve. Group the sticks in clumps, as they will also create shelter near the base of the tank.

THE SCENERY

◀ ❶ PEBBLES

You will need up to 10 pebbles of different sizes to create the undulating base of the tank. As every pebble is unique, take time to select ones which complement each other in terms of both color and shape. Make sure to choose pebbles composed of hard igneous rock, rather than soft, alkaline limestone or chalky substances.

▼ ❷ BOGWOOD

Select 3 or 4 large pieces of old bogwood which complement each other in shape and proportion. They will be used to add both height and depth, as well as providing welcome shelter for the fish. Each piece should be at least one-quarter the length of the tank.

▶ ❸ STRAIGHT TWIGS

Use a craft knife to cut straight twigs into 30 to 35 lengths, no longer than the height of the tank.

STAGE SET-UP

Lay the gravel base. Position the wood across the center of the tank with the widest ends facing the sides. Group the pebbles around the wood, building them up slightly to create crevices between them. Gather the twigs into bunches and stick between and behind the wood. Press them into the gravel to secure, allowing some to stand straight and some to lean at an angle.

▶ ❹ PEA GRAVEL

Finer than regular gravel, pea gravel is widely available from aquatic centers. It provides a solid base and helps to anchor the rocks in an upright position. For a 3 in (7.5cm) layer in a medium-sized tank, you will need about 33lb (15kg).

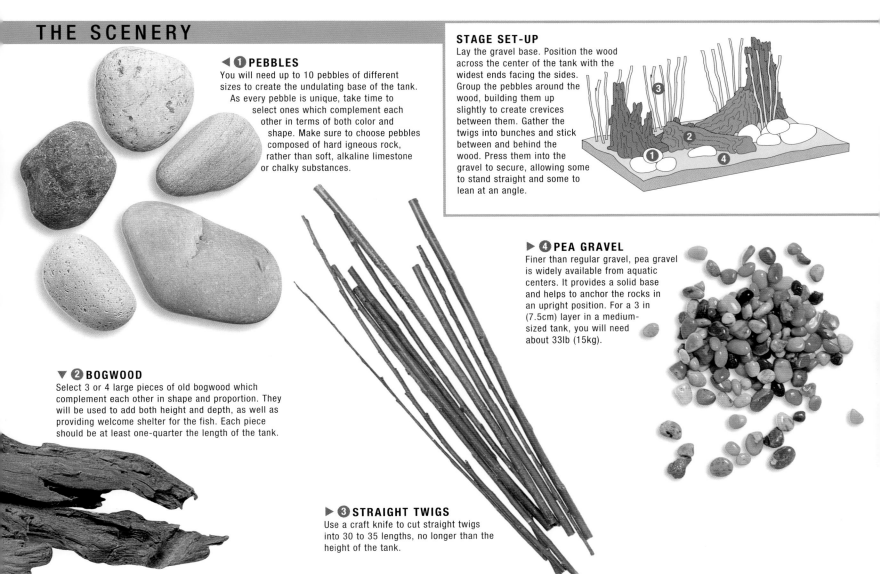

ALTERNATIVE FISH

GOLDFISH

The hardiest of fish, Goldfish are happy in cold water, so they are perfect for the first-time aquarium keeper, who does not want to worry about heaters and thermometers. Goldfish may bully other smaller fish, so it is best not to add them to tropical aquariums with more delicate fish. Use them as alternatives to Blue Coral Platies or Pimelodella pictus, but not with Neon Tetra.

NEON TETRA

The small and colorful Neon Tetra is of particular visual interest when kept in shoals of 10 or more. The blue, red, and silver colors on their bodies glow dramatically in the light of the aquarium. They can be prone to attack from larger fish, so keep them in an aquarium with other small breeds of fish. Use them on their own as alternatives to Blue Coral Platies or Pimelodella pictus.

ADD TO THE LOOK

Add real or synthetic aquarium plants to provide color variation and more shelter. The flowing leaves of Twisted Vallis, Congo Anubias, and Sword Plants add color and texture against the wood and twigs.

petrified
FOREST

Like the eerie sensation in a
haunted forest, this aquarium is a scary
place that would create the perfect
atmosphere for Halloween or a midnight ghost
story—just turn off the living room lights!

Woods in the winter can be scary places. When the leaves have
fallen from the branches, the spiny twigs can look like fingers waiting
to grab you. With a reputation for stripping a carcass to the bone
in seconds, Piranhas are able to strike fear and terror into most
people, and so are the perfect occupants for this stylish
but sinister aquarium.

THE CAST

PIRANHA
Famous for their sharp,
interlocking teeth, Piranhas are
lively and interesting fish. When young, they are
silver in color, catching the light as they dart
between the branches in this eerie aquarium.
Use 20 to 30 fish in a medium-sized tank.

• FISH CARE •
Piranhas must always be kept in a single
species tank. They will eat any other fish put
in the tank with them. They will even nip at
each other, so do not be alarmed to see
chunks and bite marks in the fish
occasionally. They can grow to a large size if
kept in the right conditions and fed properly,
so think carefully before buying them, and
do not overcrowd the tank.

ALTERNATIVE FISH

GLASS CATFISH
Glass Catfish are shy and nervous catfish,
with see-through bodies and long barbels.
They are happiest kept in small shoals of 6.
Use as an alternative to the Piranhas.

THE SCENERY

◀ ❶ ORIENTAL TWISTED WILLOW
The curved shapes of Oriental Twisted Willow's branches give a dramatic and flowing feel to the aquarium. Use 5 to 8 thin pieces for the best effect.

▼ ❷ HAIRGRASS
The thin leaves of Hairgrass will help create that spooky forest feeling. Use 4 clumps of hairgrass, split up and placed sparsely around the tank.

▼ ❸ THIN TWIGS
Use thin twigs to create the effect of leafless branches and saplings in your forest. To enhance the feeling, select twigs that are stripped of any leaves and are already dry.

▶ ❹ PEA GRAVEL
For a 3 in (7.5cm) layer in a medium-sized tank, use about 33lb (15kg) of pea gravel.

STAGE SET-UP
First, to create a slightly uneven base, lay the gravel. Then start adding the twigs so that they point vertically out of the gravel, working from the back of the tank to the front. Place in clumps together, and on their own. Plant the Hairgrass to create the effect of long grass on the forest floor in between the twigs as you go. Add the Oriental Twisted Willow between the twigs and Hairgrass.

ADD TO THE LOOK

SILVER SHARKS
Although peaceful, this is an active fish and should only be placed with fish of a similar size. Silver Sharks are also excellent jumpers, so keep the tank well sealed. Do not place more than 3 in a medium-sized tank, and only use as an alternative to the Piranhas.

Add 2 pieces of bogwood to enhance the feel of the forest floor, the pieces bringing to mind old logs and fallen trees.

black as
COAL

A bold and striking design, this tank uses a black background to enhance the natural colors of the fish and provide an eye-catching aquarium display.

The dark background brings out the color and splendor of brightly colored tropical fish. The tank is perfect for anyone who wants to make a dramatic statement. Pitch-black coal and a dark base provide a stylish, yet secure, environment for the smaller inhabitants of the aquarium, but at the same time show them off to their maximum potential.

THE SCENERY

▶ ❶ COAL

Pure black coal creates a dramatic landscape; its surface is also slightly reflective and is highlighted under the water. As a guide, choose 3 or 4 large pieces, roughly about one-quarter of the tank's length.

• COAL CARE •

Before placing the coal in the tank, scrub the pieces vigorously under cold running water. Do not use ready-packed smokeless coal fuel or barbecue coal as these contain chemical additives which will harm your fish. Refer to pages 12–13 for more information on selecting and preparing your tank scenery.

▲ ❷ BLACK GLASS CHIPPINGS

With a tinge of dark green, pre-tumbled glass chippings provide an original alternative to blackened aquarium gravel. For a 3 in (7.5cm) layer in a medium-sized tank, you will need about 33lb (15kg).

THE CAST

GOLDEN GUPPY

The small, but beautiful, Golden Guppy has very bright yellow scales and long, flowing fins, providing a unique, dramatic display. For the best results, keep only males in the tank—they look stunning in a shoal against the dark background. Use between 45 and 50 fish.

CLOWN LOACH

The orange stripes of the Clown Loach also look wonderful against the black of the coal. As bottom dwellers, Clown Loaches provide movement and excitement at the base of your tank, and are sure to enjoy hiding in the crevices in and around the coal. Use between 6 and 10 fish in the tank.

• FISH CARE •

If you want to keep both male and female Guppies, it is best to keep 4 female Guppies for every male, as the males tend to pester the females to breed, and this can exhaust a lone female.

ALTERNATIVE FISH

DWARF RAINBOW FISH

Dwarf Rainbow Fish have attractive markings and a slight metallic finish to the scales. Bright and colorful, these hardy, shoaling fish are relatively easy to keep. They will share a tank with any of the fish described on this page.

YELLOW PLATY

As Platies are somewhat larger than Guppies, fewer fish are needed to make a strong effect. These fish are also live-breeders, so a tankful of Platies will quickly produce a good number of offspring. Combine Yellow Platies with Guppies and Clown Loaches, or any of their alternatives.

BLACK RUBY BARB

The metallic red effect of the scales on the Black Ruby Barb is a brilliant contrast to the black coal, but enhances the polished edges of charcoal that refract the light. A friendly and active fish, this is a good choice for a community tank including any of the fish described on this page, or if kept in groups.

CHERRY BARB

The Cherry Barb is a small, red fish, which likes to form shoals in its natural habitat. The male's bright red scales stand out brilliantly against the black of the coal, and a shoal of 20 to 30 Cherry Barbs will look dramatic and exciting. They will live peacefully with Guppies, Clown Loaches, Dwarf Rainbow Fish, Yellow Platies, and Rosy Barbs.

ADD TO THE LOOK

STAGE SET-UP

Lay the base layer, then stand 3 pieces of coal at varying angles across the tank, using their naturally uneven shape to create alcoves between them—these will provide places of shelter for the fish. Add an extra piece of coal to the back-left corner to create a sense of depth. Press the coal into the glass flooring to secure.

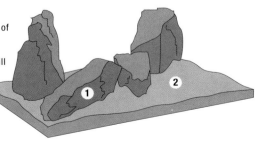

If you prefer not to use coal in your aquarium, then carefully select large pieces of bogwood and clean well before use. The wood will turn dark brown in the water so the effect of highlighting the fish will also be achieved. Synthetic aquarium wood pieces also make an effective substitute.

blue and
WHITE

An aquarium suggesting purity and peace, this blue and white tank provides the best home for graceful and delicate light blue fish, highlighted against a clean, white backdrop of white rocks and white wood.

A creative use of natural and man-made materials works well together in this tank—the rocks and wood must be strategically placed to create sufficient shelter for the fish. Color contrast is provided by the simple addition of colored paper or acrylic sheeting to the outside back of the tank.

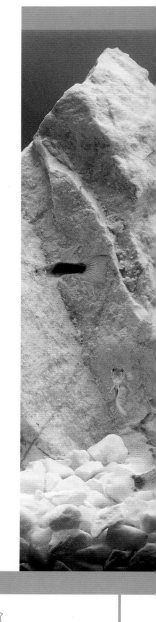

▲ ❶ WHITE ROCKS
White rocks provide a dramatic backdrop for your fish. Select 2 rocks, measuring approximately three-quarters the height of the tank, and one-quarter the length. Take care to select hard rock, such as white granite, rather than soft rock, such as limestone or other chalky or alkaline substances, as these are totally unsuitable for the fish.

▲ ❷ PAINTED BOGWOOD
You will need 1 piece of real or synthetic bogwood, measuring approximately half the height of the tank and half the length. Spray the wood all over with white, non-toxic acrylic paint, taking care to cover all the uneven areas. Seal the surface with non-toxic acrylic sealant, yacht varnish, or aquarium silicone adhesive to ensure the paint does not dissolve. Check with your aquarium store that your paint and sealant are safe to use.

THE SCENERY

▶ ❸ WHITE STONE CHIPPINGS
Use white stone chippings to create a stunning base layer for the tank. For a 3 in (7.5cm) layer in a medium-sized tank, you will need about 33lb (15kg).

STAGE SET-UP
Lay the base layer of white stone chippings. Position the painted bogwood on the right-hand side at a slight angle. Place the largest piece of rock in the center, leaning it against the wood to create a crevice. Push the rock into the stone chippings to secure. Position the second rock on the left-hand side, again burying it in the gravel for stability.

THE CAST

NEON BLUE GUPPY
The male Neon Blue Guppy is a small, attractive fish with a striking blue body and long blue fins. The long tails make a stunning display in the water, especially when the fish are kept in large numbers. If you intend to keep both male and female Guppies together, always have 4 females to every male to ensure the males do not pester an already tired female for mating. Keep between 20 and 30 Guppies in this tank.

NEON BLUE PLATY
With a bright blue body and light blue fins, both the male and female Neon Blue Platy are equally attractive. Males and females can be kept together—use about 20 in a medium-sized tank—as they look striking, and mix superbly with the colors of the Guppies.

• FISH CARE •
When using rocks with sharp edges, rub the edges of the rocks together to smooth any sharpness before placing them in the tank. Always rinse the rocks carefully and soak overnight before adding to the aquarium.

ALTERNATIVE FISH

NEON BLUE DWARF GOURAMI
Larger than the Guppies and Platies, Neon Blue Dwarf Gouramis are much more graceful, moving sedately around the blue and white tank. The male has bright blue scales, whereas the female can be duller, or even a silver hue. They are happiest when kept in male–female couples.

building
BLOCKS

A sleek and modern aquarium, this tank exploits strong shapes and stark angles of natural rock. It also provides perfect shelter and shade for the fish.

Sheer and striking, this tank is an amalgam of architectural shapes and forms. Sheets of flat stone are used to create bridges and divides that the fish will adore, while a few well-placed plants soften the overall scheme and establish a sense of color balance.

THE CAST

RED EYE TETRA
These silver Tetras have bright red eyes and a black stripe by the base of the tail. They are happiest in large groups, though tend to pick on smaller fish if kept in groups as part of a community tank. However, in a solitary shoal, they make a dazzling and effective display, while living quite peaceably with each other. You will need between 50 and 60 fish.

ALTERNATIVE FISH

DWARF RAINBOW FISH
Dwarf Rainbow Fish are bright and colorful with attractive markings, and a slight metallic finish to the scales. These hardy, shoaling fish are relatively easy to keep. Use as an alternative to the Red Eye Tetra.

ANGELFISH
Angelfish are large, elegant Cichlids with elongated fins and silver, white, and black colorings. These stately fish can be aggressive to smaller or long-finned species, so it is preferable to keep them either as a group or with other large fish.

THE SCENERY

STAGE SET-UP
Lay the base level. Starting at the back of the tank, place 1 or 2 rocks next to each other to create a wall on the left-hand side. On the right-hand side, stand 2 pieces of rock opposite each other, then place another on top to create a "roof." Leaving a gap for the plants, build up a central wall of medium-sized rocks, propping up with smaller pieces as necessary. For the bench at the front, select 2 small, square pieces on which to rest a single rectangular slab. Enclose the bench with a single piece to the left. Create a small trough for the Vallis and Cryptocoryne between the back and central walls, then carefully position the plants. Plant the Dwarf Anubias in the front-right area.

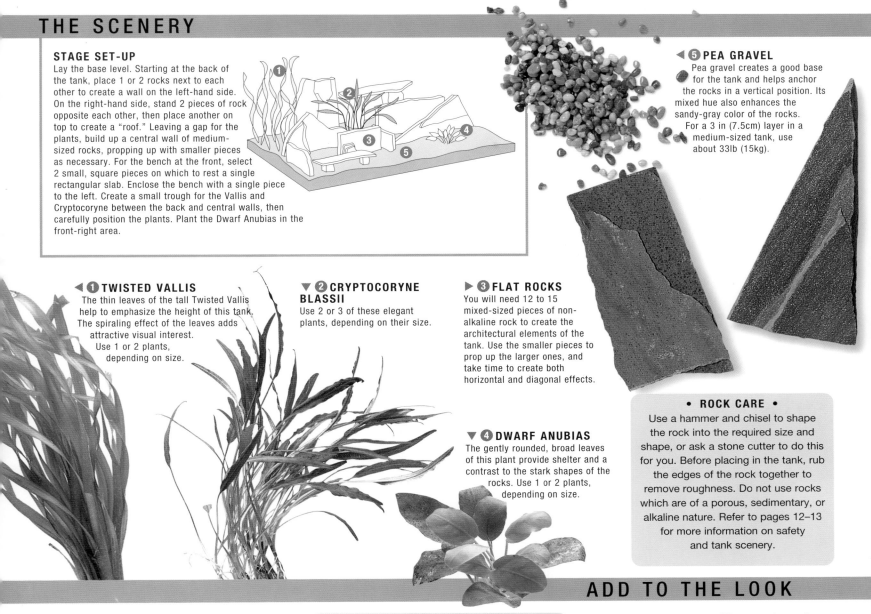

◀ ❺ PEA GRAVEL
Pea gravel creates a good base for the tank and helps anchor the rocks in a vertical position. Its mixed hue also enhances the sandy-gray color of the rocks. For a 3 in (7.5cm) layer in a medium-sized tank, use about 33lb (15kg).

◀ ❶ TWISTED VALLIS
The thin leaves of the tall Twisted Vallis help to emphasize the height of this tank. The spiraling effect of the leaves adds attractive visual interest. Use 1 or 2 plants, depending on size.

▼ ❷ CRYPTOCORYNE BLASSII
Use 2 or 3 of these elegant plants, depending on their size.

▶ ❸ FLAT ROCKS
You will need 12 to 15 mixed-sized pieces of non-alkaline rock to create the architectural elements of the tank. Use the smaller pieces to prop up the larger ones, and take time to create both horizontal and diagonal effects.

▼ ❹ DWARF ANUBIAS
The gently rounded, broad leaves of this plant provide shelter and a contrast to the stark shapes of the rocks. Use 1 or 2 plants, depending on size.

• ROCK CARE •
Use a hammer and chisel to shape the rock into the required size and shape, or ask a stone cutter to do this for you. Before placing in the tank, rub the edges of the rock together to remove roughness. Do not use rocks which are of a porous, sedimentary, or alkaline nature. Refer to pages 12–13 for more information on safety and tank scenery.

ADD TO THE LOOK

PEARL GOURAMI
Pearl Gouramis have thin, slender bodies which wonderfully complement the shape of the stone. They have distinctive markings on a dark background that filters through to the fins. Use them instead of, or combine with, the Red Eye Tetras.

• FISH CARE •
It is important that the fish have many hiding places between the rocks. Create shade by constructing tables of rock at different heights around the tank. Fish will also like to slide in between rocks that have been anchored close together, so ensure there is enough space between your rocks to allow them to maneuver freely.

You may want to use different plants in this aquarium such as Red Myriophyllum to add color. Alternatively, you could have the stone slabs pointing upward and have just a few leaning against each other to create shelter and shade. If you decide to do this, ensure that all the slabs are running parallel to the sides of the tanks so your fish remain visible.

sophisticated
SLATE

A simple, yet dramatic aquarium using dark grays, white, and greens to create an elegant sculptured feel.

As a focal element, natural slate provides stunning sharp angles to offset the natural fluidity of the plant and fish life in this tank. The depths of color of the material, and the reds and greens of the chosen plants provide a striking backdrop to the silvery white of Mollies and Gouramis.

Easy to construct and relatively low-maintenance, this tank is aimed at the aquarium owner who wants minimum fuss and maximum design effect. By providing both shelter and shade for your fish, you will gain hours of entertainment, watching them weave in and out of the foliage.

THE CAST

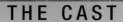

MOONLIGHT GOURAMI
These Gouramis are an elegant and peaceful addition to any tank. With their white coloring, they are perfectly displayed against the dark slate and bring out the white patches on the Mollies. They are happiest kept in male–female couples. These graceful fish are ideal for newcomers to fish keeping. Use 2 or 3 fish for a medium-sized tank.

POLKA DOT MOLLY
Mollies are live-breeders, and with both males and females in the tank you can expect to have several dozen live young within a few weeks. As the other fish are likely to eat the young, you may choose to use a fish trap or breeding tank when the females fall pregnant. Ask at your aquarium store for details on using these products. You will need 4 to 6 fish for a medium-sized tank.

• FISH CARE •
As for all tropical aquariums, make sure the tank is heated and oxygenated sufficiently before use. Take care not to overcrowd the tank. Even with sufficient filtration and oxygenation, an overcrowded tank will make the fish uncomfortable.

THE SCENERY

◀ ❶ RED AND WHITE DRACENA

The broad, reddish leaves of this plant provide a sense of contrast with the thin, narrow leaves of the wheat plant. It also gives the fish extra cover when seeking shelter from light or other fish. Use 1 or 2 plants.

STAGE SET-UP

Lay the gravel base. Choose 2 or 3 slate slabs to lay horizontally near the front of the tank, and taller pieces to stand upright at the back. Place the Red and White Dracena, and Arrowhead to the right of the tank between the slate slabs. Position the Wheat Plant on the left-hand side, interleaving the plants between the slate.

▼ ❹ WHITE GRAVEL

White gravel provides a good base and helps anchor plants and rocks. Its pale gray shading highlights the darkness of the slate. Wash well before use to remove any dust and impurities. For a 3 in (7.5cm) layer in a medium-sized tank, you'll need about 33lb (15kg).

▶ ❺ SLATE

This versatile material can be trimmed and shaped as required, and positioned in a variety of ways within the aquarium environment. For a medium-sized tank, you will need about 6 slabs, depending on size. Each piece should be no larger than one-third the length of the tank.

▶ ❷ WHEAT PLANT

Wheat Plant introduces an angular viewpoint to the tank. Its vivid color contrasts well with the slate and mimics the natural lines within the rock. Use 4 to 6 plants, depending on size.

◀ ❸ ARROWHEAD

Also known as Crow Foot or Goose Foot, this pretty plant has shapely, deep green leaves which give the fish plenty of cover. The strong, thin stems make the plant easy to position and secure. Use 1 or 2 plants for a medium-sized tank.

• SLATE CARE •

Before filling your tank, sand the edges of the slate together to smooth off any sharp edges that may harm the fish. Also, soak the slate in water for a few days to ensure any pollutants are removed. Refer to pages 12–13 for more information on preparing your tank scenery.

ALTERNATIVE FISH

ANGELFISH

Pair the elegant Angelfish, with its silver, white, and black coloring, and the Red Eye Tetra for a stunning alternative to the Gourami and Molly combination.

RED EYE TETRA

This large silver fish with red eyes lives happily with the more aggressive Angelfish.

ADD TO THE LOOK

You could introduce various Mollies which have an attractive black and white color scheme, such as the Chocolate Marble Sailfin or the Green Sailfin Molly. Albino Catfish would continue the white theme, and also help clean the tank by eating excess food.

Other plants which go well with slate include Giant Indian Water Star, Bamboo, Twisted Vallis, Java Fern, and Hairgrass. Add interest by dropping in pieces of pure coal, which have been scrubbed clean.

red
ALL OVER

A daring and flamboyant tank, this red-themed aquarium could be something from the planet Mars and will create a rich focal point in any room.

This minimal landscape is created using a host of red props: granite rock, a painted disc, and stones. The plants also have a reddish theme: Ivy, Ludwigia, and Alternanthera. The fish chosen for this tank will swim in the middle waters and are beautifully framed by the backdrop. Keep the lighting relatively subdued.

THE CAST

CHERRY BARBS
These very bright red fish will dart around this aquarium happily. Use no more than 10 fish in a medium-sized tank.

NEON ROSY BARBS
Slightly larger than the Cherry Barbs, Neon Rosy Barbs are extremely easy to keep and ideal for beginners. The dramatic effect of the scales reflects a rainbow of colors in the light. They are active and friendly fish that will provide huge amounts of interest. Use no more than 20 in a medium-sized tank.

ALTERNATIVE FISH

HONEY GOURAMI
Graceful and elegant, Honey Gourami are medium sized and are a light orange color. The male Honey Gourami turns dark blue when threatened by other fish. Best kept in male–female pairs. Use as an alternative to Barbs rather than as an addition; they are better kept as a single species.

THE SCENERY

◀ ❶ POLISHED RED STONES
Select 2 polished red stones to fill the foreground area of the aquarium.

▲ ❷ RED STONES
Select worn pieces of red brick for the base of the tank. Soak the bricks in a weak bleach solution for at least 1 day to remove impurities. Rinse continuously in clean water until the bleach smell is totally removed. Use 33lb (15kg) stones for a medium-sized tank.

◀ ❸ RED GRANITE ROCKS
Use 2 chunks of dappled, red granite to create a stunning landscape. Choose pieces that are about one-third the length of the tank.

▼ ❹ ALTERNANTHERA ROSAEFOLIA
Use 2 or 3 of these purple plants in the left-hand corner of the tank.

◀ ❺ RED DISC
A single red disc, about one-third the length of the tank, gives the impression of a slowly-setting sun. It should be made of plastic or wood and painted with a non-toxic acrylic paint. If necessary, saw off the base to level the surface. Smooth the cut surface with wet-dry paper, then seal with non-toxic acrylic sealant. Leave to dry for at least 2 days.

▼ ❻ RED LUDWIGIA
You'll need 2 or 3 examples of this tall red plant.

▼ ❼ GIANT RED IVY
A strong corner prop, the Giant Red Ivy provides essential shelter for the fish. Use 2 or 3 plants.

STAGE SET-UP
Start by positioning the granite rocks. Place the first on the left-hand side of the tank. Place the second, larger piece to the right. Position the disc on the back wall slightly off center between the two rocks, then cover the floor of the tank with red stones to keep the rocks and disc firmly in position. Plant the Giant Red Ivy in the right-hand back corner. Plant the Red Ludwigia between the disc and the large rock, and the two Altenantheras, one to the right in front of the large rock, the other to the left behind the upright rock. Add larger pebble-shaped red stones around the base of the rocks, and finish off with two highly polished stones in front of the upright one.

ADD TO THE LOOK

SERPAE TETRA
This scarlet fish has black patterning and an attractive profile. Serpae Tetras are best kept in small numbers, since they have a tendency to become aggressive when kept in groups.

HARLEQUIN RASBORA
These small, attractive red fish sport a distinctive black triangle on their sides. Lively and amusing, Harlequins are relatively easy to keep and are happiest in groups of 4 or more.

• FISH CARE •
Soak the granite in water for at least 2 days before adding to the aquarium to ensure any possible salt or chemical pollutants are washed away thoroughly. Refer to pages 12–13 for more information on preparing tank scenery.

For more interest, you could add Red-Clawed Thai Crabs, which would help keep the tank clean by feasting on leftover food and algae. There is a wide selection of artificial plants that will intensify the red theme of your tank. Ask at your aquarium store for details.

arctic
DREAMSCAPE

A freezing, silver-white dreamscape. This is actually a mix of frosty white, pink, and blue crystals.

Almost ice-like in appearance, this crystal aquarium could be a frozen scene from the Arctic tundra, or perhaps C.S. Lewis's magical land of Narnia. The crystals' delicate colors are enhanced by the clear water and aquarium light. The stunningly cool, yet beautiful, jeweled appearance entrances the viewer, yet its frosty remoteness will always seem like some distant constellation. The white base and delicate shades of pink and blue will help your dark fish stand out dramatically for all to see.

THE CAST

GOLD GOURAMI
The elegant Gold Gourami complements the graceful Angelfish, and is large enough not to be threatened by its companions. The beautiful, subtle markings of this fish will show up to full effect against the pale background. You will need between 8 and 10 fish in total.

BLACK MARBLE ANGELFISH
The pale colors of this crystal setting show off the Black Marble Angelfish in its full glory. The jet-black, jagged outlines are conspicuous against the pink and blue crystals, as well as casting stunning reflections on the rock itself. You will need between 10 and 12 fish.

• FISH CARE •
Be sure to use tumbled glass, otherwise the fish may scratch themselves. If this is not available, smooth the edges yourself with wet-dry sandpaper, then rinse well before use. Refer to pages 12–13 for more information on safety and preparing your tank scenery.

THE SCENERY

▼ ❶ ROUGH CRYSTALS

Add color and texture with rough pink and blue crystals. Use up to 8 mixed rock crystals—for a medium-sized tank, the pieces should be 1 in to 4 in (2.5cm to 10cm) in diameter. For the main blue crystal, select a large geode measuring about 8 in (20cm) in diameter, or up to one-third the length of the tank. Remember to smooth off the edges slightly before use.

◀ ❷ LARGE WHITE CRYSTAL

Choose 1 large piece of white or clear crystal, such as quartz to create a focal point on the side of the tank. Its size can be up to one-third the length of the tank. Smooth off sharp edges slightly before use.

◀ ❸ POLISHED PINK CRYSTALS

For depth of color and a smooth contrast, add about six polished, pink crystals, such as rose quartz or rock crystal. For a medium-sized tank, these should be no larger than 4 in (10cm) in diameter.

▶ ❹ WHITE GLASS CHIPPINGS

Made from recycled, tumbled glass, these opaque chippings mingle with the delicate crystals, while providing a solid color base. Make sure to wash well before placing in the tank. For a 3 in (7.5cm) layer in a medium tank, you'll need about 33lb (15kg) chippings.

STAGE SET-UP

Lay the glass base in an uneven manner, building up the chippings on either side of the tank. Position the large blue crystal on the left and the white crystal to the right. Arrange the smaller rough crystals around the blue crystal across the center. Arrange the polished pink crystals in front of the white crystal. If your tank is against a wall, you may like to create extra contrast by securing a piece of blue acrylic or plastic to the back, cut to size.

ALTERNATIVE FISH

BLACK WIDOW

Black Widows make handsome alternatives or additions to Black Marble Angelfish. Their silver and black bodies with 3 black stripes down the side will stand out clearly against the bright background of your tank.

BLACK MOLLY

Black Mollies look dramatic against these stunning surroundings. Best kept in male–female couples, these friendly and lively fish create an eye-catching display when kept in groups of 10 or more. They can be combined with any of the other fish suggested for this tank.

ADD TO THE LOOK

You could use even more crystals to add height and drama to this tank. Build the crystals up the side of your tank for a more cavernous appearance. Artificially colored quartz is produced in a wide range of colors, such as gold, purple, and yellow, if you prefer different effects.

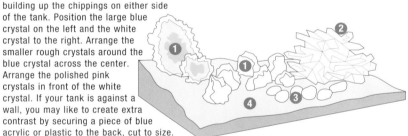

fossil
DISCOVERY

This atmospheric aquarium with its collection of ancient fossils conjures up images of an archaeological excavation. While the scenery evokes the dreamy feeling of being suspended in time, the Shark Catfish and Red Tiger Oscars hint at a wilder prehistoric age.

Using fossils bought from a natural history museum or mineral supplier, you can create an effective centerpiece around ancient bones, shells, and plant remains. If you look carefully, you may be lucky enough to find a fossil that still retains an impression of a piscine creature from thousands of years ago.

THE CAST

RED TIGER OSCAR

Strongly patterned Cichlids, Red Tiger Oscars are particularly beautiful fish, and they become even more decorative with age. Similar to other Oscars in habit, they are highly aggressive toward other fish in the aquarium. Although they are often kept in single species tanks, they can be successfully combined with other strong-willed fish, such as the Shark Catfish. Use 16 or 17 Red Tiger Oscars in a medium-sized tank.

SHARK CATFISH

The Shark Catfish earns its name by looking and swimming in a manner usually only seen in much larger ocean-dwelling sharks. In their natural habitat, however, this variety can also grow very large. Shark Catfish can be aggressive to other fish so they need to be combined with fish that are equally aggressive. Use 2 or 3 Shark Catfish in a medium-sized tank.

• FISH CARE •

As Shark Catfish naturally migrate to sea as they get larger, you will need to add a small amount of aquarium salt to the water as the fish get older in order to mimic this migratory pattern. Ask your local aquarium dealer for more information on this topic when you buy your fish.

THE SCENERY

• SLATE AND FOSSIL CARE •
Before filling your tank, sand the edges of the slate and the fossils to smooth off any sharp edges that may harm the fish. Also soak all of the fossils and the slate in water for a few days to ensure any pollutants are removed. Refer to pages 12–13 for more information on preparing your tank scenery.

▶ ❶ SILICA SAND
Laying silica sand on the base of this aquarium will help anchor the fossils in place. For a 3 in (7.5cm) layer in a medium-sized tank, you'll need about 45lb (20kg).

▼ ❷ TWISTED VALLIS
The long, thin leaves of the Twisted Vallis plant flow gently behind the fossils and provide height in this tank. Use 2 to 3 plants, depending on size.

▼ ❸ CRYPTOCORYNE CILIATA
Any plant in the Cryptocoryne family will suit this tank, as its leaves provide a good contrast to the large ammonite. Use 1 to 2 plants.

▼ ❹ FOUNTAIN PLANT
With its slim, dark green leaves, the Fountain Plant provides low-level shelter for the fish. Use 1 to 2 plants, depending on size.

◀ ❺ FOSSILS
You will need 1 large ammonite measuring one-third the length of the tank, 4 smaller ammonites, 1 fossilized fish specimen, and 1 piece of slate with embedded fossils. Check the rock type before buying your fossils, and avoid all soft, chalky, or alkaline specimens.

▶ ❻ WATER WISTERIA
The frilly leaves of this plant contrast with the hardness of the fossil rock and provide plenty of shelter for the fish. Use 1 or 2 plants, depending on size.

STAGE SET-UP
Lay the sand base. Place the large ammonite just left of center. Add the smaller ammonites in front and to the right. Position the fish fossil on the right-hand side of the tank. Put the fossilized slate centrally toward the back of the tank. Plant the Twisted Vallis in the right-hand back corner, and place the Fountain Plants just in front, behind the fish fossil. Plant the Water Wisteria in the left-hand back corner. Finally, plant the Cryptocoryne at the back in the center, behind the slate.

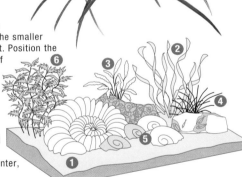

ALTERNATIVE FISH

WHIPTAILED CATFISH
This long, elegant Catfish matches the natural tones of the ancient scenery and makes an ideal alternative to the Shark Catfish. You will need no more than 2 fish in the tank.

GLASS CATFISH
The Glass Catfish has a transparent body, making its skeleton clearly visible. Perfect for a tank dedicated to fossils, the Glass Catfish looks like a fossilized, but mobile animal itself. A nervous fish, it is best kept in groups of 6 or more as a single species. It would be inadvisable to keep this fish with the Red Tiger Oscars, Shark Catfish, or Whiptail Catfish.

ADD TO THE LOOK

You may wish to scatter a few cleaned shells and small rocks among the fossils to give your display a "then and now" effect. For a background color, cut a piece of thick red card or acrylic sheeting to the length and height of your tank. Using adhesive tape, stick it firmly to the outside back wall of your tank.

jeweled
CAVERN

Rich and sumptuous, this cavern-style aquarium forms a colorful centerpiece in any room. Purple glass flooring and reddish plants add to the intensity of color, while Lavender Gouramis enjoy the numerous retreats created in the tank environment.

The natural colors of agate and amethyst are brought to life under the bright light of the aquarium environment. The clear water complements the jeweled effect of the gemstones, making every facet sparkle.

The amethyst's coloring is caused by tiny traces of iron in the gem's structure, while the hollow of the agate is formed by a bubble in basaltic lava. The concentric color bands in the agate are formed by traces of iron and manganese, although these can be enhanced by synthetic coloring.

THE CAST

LAVENDER GOURAMI

The pale coloring of the Lavender Gourami is enhanced by the rich hues of the agate and the beautiful surroundings. The hints of iridescence on their subtle, lavender scales glimmer, as the fish turn slowly in the water. Use 10 to 12 fish for a medium-sized tank.

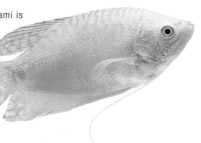

• FISH CARE •

As the edges of the agate are not smooth, it is important to choose fish that will not spend too much time near the base of the aquarium. Do not keep bottom feeders in this type of tank as they will scratch themselves on the rocks. Refer to pages 12–13 for details on fish safety.

ALTERNATIVE FISH

PINK KISSING GOURAMI

Kissing Gouramis are pale pink in color, with a very lighter tinge to their scales. The males battle for the attention of the females and for territory within the tank. They wrestle each other with their mouths, giving rise to their poetic name. For a medium-sized tank, you will need 10 to 15 fish, depending on maturity.

THE SCENERY

▶ ❶ AGATE AND AMETHYST GEODES
Agate and amethyst geodes look like regular rocks from the outside but reveal wonderful caves of delight when split open. The amethyst (below) is filled with alcoves of purple crystals, while the agate (right) reveals characteristic bands of color. When choosing, select pieces which are no larger than one-third the length of the tank and three-quarters its depth. Smooth off the rough edges with wet-dry sandpaper before use.

STAGE SET-UP
Lay the glass base, building up the chippings slightly to the back and sides. Position the agate on the left, and the amethyst on the right, taking care that their interior patterns are clearly visible. Place the plants just off-center, keeping them in their original growing pots to protect the roots. If your tank is to be positioned against a wall, you may like to create a dramatic finish by securing a sheet of shot purple paper or silk fabric to the back of the tank.

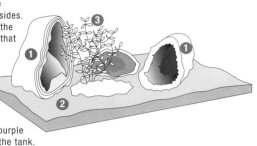

• PLANT CARE •
To protect the roots and make the plants easier to handle, remember to keep them in their planting pots as you place them in the tank.
As the plant is colored, the fresh shoots on the Red Ludwigia will be green. Replace the plant as necessary.

▶ ❷ PURPLE GLASS CHIPPINGS
These tumbled glass chippings enhance the natural colors of the agate and amethyst, and at the same time provide a solid base layer for the tank. For a 3 in (7.5cm) layer in a medium-sized tank, you will need about 33lb (15kg). Always use ready-tumbled glass or smooth off the edges before use.

▶ ❸ RED LUDWIGIA
The reddish-purple leaves of Red Ludwigia help to complement the agate and glass chippings, while providing some useful hiding spaces and shelter for the fish. You'll need 1 large plant, or 2 to 3 medium-sized plants.

ADD TO THE LOOK

ALBINO PANGASIUS
With its characteristic barbels around the mouth, this pale pink fish adds plenty of dramatic movement to the tank. An albino version of Pangasius sutchi, or Asian Shark Catfish, it needs plenty of space to swim and roam. Do not place more than 2 of these fish in a medium-sized tank.

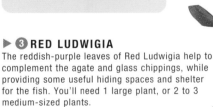

Use different varieties of plant life to contrast with the purple agate. Light green plants such as Myriophyllum or Arrowhead tend to stand out most effectively against the purple.

color
FRENZY

A colorful and exciting kaleidoscope of
multi-hued plants and fish helps to create
a vibrant community tank with a difference.

A wild and stimulating combination of plants and fish
brings this vivid tank to life. Its multi-colored platies are totally
spoiled by the variety of plants they have to enjoy, while the
plants themselves make a stunning display in their own right.

THE CAST

ALTERNATIVE FISH

GUPPY
Guppies are also available in a range of
colors, and are ideal as an addition or
alternative to the Platies. They will make
the most of the dense planting, and breed
heavily. Remove fry to a separate
tank, otherwise
they'll be eaten.

NEON TETRA
Tiny, colorful fish, Neon Tetras are one of
the most popular breeds amongst aquarium
owners. Kept in groups of 6 or more, they
can provide an exciting shoal of vibrant
reds and blues as they speed around the
aquarium. Being small and conspicuous,
they tend to be preyed upon by larger fish.

HIGH-FIN PLATIES
Use a mix of Platies in this tank to contrast with the plant
life. You will need 15 to 20 fish for a medium-sized tank.

THE SCENERY

▼ **①** PYGMY CHAIN SWORD PLANT
Use 8 plants to fill out the front of the tank.

▲ **②** RED LOBELIA
Use 4 or 5 clumps of Red Lobelia to lift the color at the front of the planting arrangement.

▶ **③** BOGWOOD
Select 1 piece of bogwood to stand on the left of the tank, among the plants.

▶ **⑨** PEA GRAVEL
Aquarium gravel is essential for anchoring the plants and rocks in this tank. For a 3 in (7.5cm) layer in a medium-sized tank, you will need about 33lb (15kg).

▶ **④** DWARF AMAZON SWORD PLANT
A good, all-around plant for the central area. Use 3 plants.

▶ **⑩** INDIAN FERN
This light-loving plant plant ranges from a dark to pale green depending on the amount of light available. Use 2 to 3 plants, depending on size.

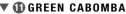

◀ **⑤** DRIED FERNS
Red, green, and orange ferns add bulk to the background plant scenery and contrast well with the greenery. Use 5 ferns.

▶ **⑥** BABY TEARS
With its delicate, tiny leaves, this plant fills out the central section of the planted area.

▼ **⑪** GREEN CABOMBA
Use 1 or 2 Cabomba plants for the center of the stage set.

◀ **⑦** NITELLA
With its shrub-like appearance, Nitella adds texture and contrast throughout the tank. Use 4 plants.

◀ **⑧** WATER STAR
Use 2 to 3 of these slim-stemmed plants to fill out the planting background.

▶ **⑫** STRAIGHT VALLIS
Use 5 to 7 plants to create the backdrop for the other plants.

SWORDTAIL
Male Swordtails have an elongated tail fin which makes them easy to spot. They often have black stripes on the fins and can look very striking. Good for a community tank, Swordtails are live-breeders and have all the same qualities as Guppies, Mollies, and Platies.

• FISH CARE •
These fish all look at their best when the fluorescent lighting reflects off their dramatic colors. Provide plenty of hiding spaces so that the fish can escape the glare of the lights if they want to relax.

STAGE SET-UP
Lay the gravel base and place the wood just off the center on the left. Lay out all the plants in order of height, since this will determine the order of planting. Use the Straight Vallis for the back corners of the tank. Place the Cabomba in the center back area. Use the mid-height plants in the central area: the Nitella, Dwarf Amazon Sword Plant, Dried Fern, Indian Fern, and Baby Tears. For the front area, use the Red Lobelia and Pygmy Chain Sword Plant.

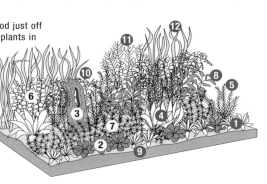

river
VALLEY

Created from striped rock, synthetic ferns, and a ceramic pagoda, this inspired landscape creates an Oriental vista for peaceful Harlequins and Purple Emperors.

The secret ingredient in this tank is modeler's polystyrene: it is easy to carve and paint, and is ideal for the planting of plastic ferns. The simplicity of the design is the key to its success: two gently curving "hillsides" frame the ceramic pagoda, which acts as a central prop in the design. Striped rock adds a natural element and suggests a cliff formation on the edge of the "hillside." The uniformity of the landscape is the perfect backdrop for the fish, whose subtle markings are highlighted by the green ferns.

THE CAST

HARLEQUIN RASBORA
These small and active free swimmers are a delight in any tank. The red coloring and black triangle at the back of the fish creates a very definite impression and their fiesty nature will amuse all who watch. For this tank you will need 20 Harlequins.

PURPLE EMPERORS
This hybrid of the regular Emperor has a distinctive purple coloration that looks striking in this simple environment. Small and active, Purple Emperors will add interest and variety to your aquarium. Use no more than 15 in a medium-sized tank.

ALTERNATIVE FISH

NEON TETRA
The blue, red, and silver flashes on these tiny fish will look stunning as they shoal with their companions across this stylish landscape. Use as an alternative to the Harlequins or Emperors.

GLOWLIGHT TETRA
With their small, but colorful bodies these fish will help add visual interest to the tank. Use as an alternative to the Harlequins and Emperors.

THE SCENERY

► ❶ SCULPTURED "HILLSIDES"

You will need: blocks of dense modeler's polystyrene; PVA wood adhesive; a craft knife; fine-toothed saw or polystyrene cutter; a small surform; wet-dry paper; small paintbrush; non-toxic green and black acrylic paint; 2 varieties of plastic fern plants.

Glue the polystyrene blocks together to form 2 rough "hills." Once the adhesive is dry, cut the sides to fit squarely against the tank walls. Use the knife and surform to shape the slopes. Carve a deep indentation in the right-hand "hill," in which to fit the larger stone. Check that the "hills" fit easily inside the tank. Once you are happy with the shape of the "hills," use the surform and wet-dry paper to smooth the edges. Use the black paint to color the outside flat edges and the indentations made for the stones. Use green paint to color the slopes.

Remove the plastic ferns from their base mat. Pierce holes in the "hillsides" with a fine knitting needle, then insert the individual fern stalks until the area is densely covered. Group the different varieties of fern to add interest to the planted area.

modeler's polystyrene

surform

part-finished "hills"

wood adhesive

wet-dry sandpaper

waterproof acrylic paint

plastic fern plants

◄ ❷ CERAMIC PAGODA

Use a glazed ceramic pagoda as the central prop in the tank.

▲ ❸ BLACK AND WHITE ROCKS

You will need 2 black and white aquarium rocks to create the "cliff" effect on the edge of the "hillside" and add interest to the river valley.

► ❹ SILICA SAND

Use silica sand to simulate the river bed in front of the "hills." For a medium-sized tank, use about 22lb (10kg).

STAGE SET-UP

Glue the the "hills" to the base and side of the tank using aquarium silicone adhesive. Make sure that there are no gaps where the polystyrene meets the tank, since the fish could become trapped in any gaps. Allow to dry for 2 days. Lay the sand in the "valley" to simulate the river bed. Place the pagoda at the back of the tank behind the left "hill." Fit the larger rock in the carved indentation in the right-hand "hillside" to form the "cliff." Stand the smaller rock in the center of the valley towards the front.

ADD TO THE LOOK

CHERRY BARBS

These lively red fish contrast well with the pagoda and make an ideal alternative to the Purple Emperors.

• FISH CARE •

To ensure that your fish do not swim into danger, make sure that the polystyrene is glued firmly into place and that all gaps around the sides and base of the tank are sealed up. Take care when carving the "hillsides" and make sure they sit flush to the tank wall before you start painting the surface.

To add more interest to the tank scenery, you could add taller plastic or real aquarium plants to the "hillside" to give the illusion of forests. You can also change the shape of the valley to create more of a mountain range effect with a mix of smaller and higher slopes.

capri
CAVE

The island of Capri in Italy is famed for its blue stone caves. Now, with a little imagination and some careful crafting, you can re-create that look in your own home.

Modeler's polystyrene is used to create fun and eye-catching scenery for the colorful fish in this tank. The polystyrene is easy to carve with a craft knife and can be fashioned to your own particular design.

THE CAST

BLOND RED GUPPY
The bright orange and red coloring of the Blond Red Guppy, along with its beautifully elegant tail, makes it the perfect fish to show off the richness of your blue caves. Use 10 to 15 in a medium-sized tank.

GOLDEN BARB
The highly reflective scales on the small Golden Barb adds a subtle level of visual drama to the tank. Use 10 to 15 in a medium-sized tank.

HARLEQUIN RASBORA
The black triangle at the base of the Harlequin's dorsal fin creates a stark color contrast to the scenery. The red front half of the fish complements the Blond Red Guppies and shows up well against the blue scenery. Use 10 to 15 of the fish in a medium-sized tank.

THE SCENERY

▼ ❶ POLYSTYRENE CAVE

To make the scenery, you will need: blocks of dense modeler's polystyrene; a craft knife, fine-toothed saw or polystyrene cutter; PVA wood adhesive; a small surform; wet-dry paper; a paintbrush; 2 shades of metallic acrylic paint; and plastic fern plants.

Start by gluing the blocks of polystyrene together to get the basic shape. You can build up separate sections, as here, to create the cave, or carve it out once your structure is complete. When the glue is dry, carve the peaks and cave into a freeform shape. Use the craft knife and surform for the initial carving, then wet-dry paper for a smooth surface.

Color your structure with different shades of blue paint. Use metallic paint to give the caves a sparkling finish.

Separate the plastic fern plants from their bases, make holes in the polystyrene with a fine knitting needle, then poke your plastic plants firmly into the holes.

modeler's polystyrene

wet-dry sandpaper

wood adhesive

surform

matt and metallic acrylic paint

plastic fern plants

cave base sections

cave base and middle section

◀ ❸ COLORED GLASS PEBBLES

Use a selection of blue and green, opaque and clear mixed glass pebbles to suggest the river in front of the cave. You will need around 1lb (500gms).

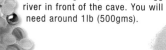

▶ ❹ SILICA SAND

For a medium-sized tank, use around 45 lbs (20kg) of silica sand on the base of the tank to cover the bottom of the Capri caves, and keep the plants in place.

▼ ❷ PYGMY CHAIN SWORD PLANT

Use 3 Pygmy Chain Sword Plants alongside the artificial plants to provide more realism. Position them near the front of the tank.

▶ ❺ DWARF SAGITTARIA

Use 2 Dwarf Sagittaria to position around the modelled caves.

STAGE SET-UP

Glue your cave (with plastic plants already added) to the base of the tank using aquarium silicone adhesive. Allow at least 48 hours for the glue to cure. Lay the sand, then plant the Pygmy Chain Sword Plants and the Dwarf Sagittaria around the front of the cave. Finish with a river of mixed blue and green glass pebbles running through the cave to the front of the aquarium.

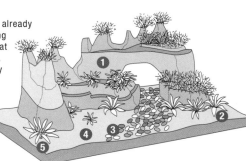

ALTERNATIVE FISH

CARDINAL TETRA

The beautiful Cardinal Tetra, with its blue-green stripe and stunning red underside adds drama when it shoals in groups. The strong colors show up particularly well against the blue caves. Use 15 to 20 fish as alternative cast members.

GLOWLIGHT TETRA

The Glowlight Tetra has a distinctive red line running along its see-through body. Similar to the Cardinal Tetras, these fish shoal in spectacular fashion when kept in groups.

• FISH CARE •
Check with your aquarium store than all of your scenery and modeling materials are suitable for the fish you use in the tank.

ADD TO THE LOOK

You may wish to add extra facets to this tank, perhaps by including a small shipwreck near the base of the rocks. Alternatively, a small sunken Italian building or sculpture would create the impression that the sea has risen quickly and engulfed a beachside building.

submarine
GROTTO

Inspired by the underwater caves of a fantasy dreamworld, this aquarium is a dramatic combination of color and texture. Hiding places keep your fish safe and satisfied.

Basic modeling materials—chicken wire and polymer clay—are used to shape the scenery of this underwater wonderland. Different shades of polymer clay are rolled together to create swirling bands of color, then rolled out and used to cover simple wire structures. After baking the component parts, the structures are then assembled in the tank and surrounded with free-flowing plants to soften the effect.

THE CAST

GREEN TIGER BARBS
These active and attractive fish are a welcome addition to any tank. The greenish body and red fins stand out wonderfully against the creams and browns of the scenery. Do not use more than 20 in a medium-sized tank, since these Barbs quarrel with other community fish.

RED PLATY
These lively and colorful fish are both inquisitive and playful, providing a constant show. The Red Platy is a variation of the original olive-green and white coloring, and this tank is stocked with just the females. Use about 10 in a medium-sized tank.

ALTERNATIVE FISH

CARDINAL TETRA
When kept in groups, these bold fish shoal dramatically. Like the Barbs, Tetras enjoy the middle water layers. Reduce the lighting and increase the plant life if using these fish.

GLOWLIGHT TETRA
This fish enjoys soft, slightly acidic water, and peat filtration. It enjoys the lower levels of the aquarium, and will take full advantage of the plant and "cave" shelter.

THE SCENERY

▶ **1 POLYMER CLAY GROTTO**

For the scenery, you will need: chicken wire; polymer clay in a selection of brown, beige, and stone-effect colors; wire cutters; protective gloves; rolling pin. Wearing the gloves, cut, then bend the wire into shapes to form the basic structure of the grotto. Cut holes in the grotto formations, trimming the wire as necessary. Roll out the polymer clay until ⅛ in (4mm) thick, mixing the colors to create stripes and swirls. Use the clay to cover the wire structures, taking care that the wire is completely sealed and there are no gaps in the covering layer. Form "scales" and "ridges" with small pieces of clay, and attach to the grotto formations to create a sense of texture and depth. Bake the component parts of the grotto following the manufacturer's instructions.

▶ **5 PEA GRAVEL**

For a medium-sized tank, use 33lb (15kg) gravel for a 3 in (7.5cm) layer.

▼ **4 STRAIGHT VALLIS**

The long, thin leaves of this plant provides essential height planted in the crevices of the scenery. Use 2 plants.

▼ **6 GREEN CABOMBA**

The delicate leaves of this plant can be seen through holes in the "caves," increasing the appeal of the overall design. Use 2 plants.

▼ **2 APONOGETON UNDULATUS**

This rhizome plant offsets the scenery and provides shelter for the fish. Use 2 plants.

▼ **3 RED LUDWIGIA**

The red color of this plant helps to emphasize the colors of the "caves." It also adds visual interest at the front of the tank. Use 2 plants.

ADD TO THE LOOK

• FISH CARE •

To ensure that the chicken wire does not rust and pollute the water, make sure that the polymer clay covers the metal completely, so that water cannot get in.

You could add to the look of this tank by changing the way you build the "caves." You could create a more traditional-looking structure with a deep cavern in the center, then plant around the outside of the cave. A selection of pebbles provides a beach effect.

STAGE SET-UP

Lay the gravel base. Place the "caves" along the center of the tank, experimenting with the arrangement until you are satisfied. Push the "caves" into the gravel slightly to secure. Plant the Red Ludwigia on the right-hand side in front of the scenery. Plant the Cabomba on the left-hand side behind the scenery. Plant the Vallis on the left-hand side between the scenery. Finally, plant the Aponogeton Undulatus between the "caves" in the center of the tank.

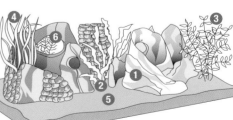

desert
OASIS

This aquarium may well be the oasis in the
desert that your fish have been searching
for—it creates the impression of a real desert,
but totally submerged under water.

The original mixing of organic striped rocks with plastic cacti
proves surprisingly effective in an aquarium that may well cause
raised eyebrows at first, but is bound to amuse and enthrall
your friends. With its exciting and enjoyable ideas, the desert oasis tank
is great for a fish owner who lives in a cold climate.

THE CAST

GOLD RAM
The attractive Gold Ram has a stunning
golden body with a red nose and blue
tinges to its scales that only show up as
the fish turns in the light. They are
territorial fish, but
generally remain
peaceful once their
territory has been
established. Use 20 fish
for a medium-sized tank.

ARCHED CATFISH
The pretty Arched Catfish has a cream body
with a long black stripe running down its back.
As with all bottom-dwellers, these fish are
perfect for keeping the floor of this tank clear
of unwanted food, as well as adding interest to
the sand. Use 20 fish for a medium-sized tank.

• FISH CARE •
Make sure that there are plenty of hiding
places for the Arched Catfish to escape
from the bullying tendencies of the Gold
Ram. Rocks with crevices and plastic
succulents will provide shelter for the more
timid fish to conceal themselves. The more
open spaces in the tank can then be
claimed by the territorial Gold Rams.

THE SCENERY

▼ ❶ PLASTIC CACTI

Traditionally used in terraria, these plastic cacti have soft spikes that will not damage your fish. You will need 6 cacti in total: 1 Succulent Rose, 1 Prickly Pear, 3 tall cacti with leaves, and 1 cactus with a round head and long prickles.

► ❷ STRIPED ROCKS

These specialist aquarium rocks mimic the desert landscape and bring the tank to life. Select 5 rocks of various sizes: from one-eighth to one-quarter the length of the tank. For the 2 largest pieces, select rocks with holes, as the fish will enjoy swimming through them. Synthetic aquarium rocks can be used as an alternative.

STAGE SET-UP

Lay the sand base. Position the 2 large rocks with holes: place 1 in the right-hand back corner and the other on the left-hand side, a little further forward. Place the 3 remaining rocks further to the front, leaving a gap in the center. Position the Prickly Pear behind the large rock and the Succulent Rose in front. Stand the 3 tall cacti in a diagonal line, from the center back to the right. Place the round-headed cactus off-center between the rocks on the left. Create a path of gravel through the middle of the tank, widening from the back to the front.

• ROCK CARE •

Although these rocks are specifically for aquariums be sure to check for sharp edges before filling your tank. Also wash the rocks well in water to remove any dust. Refer to pages 12–13 for more information on preparing your tank scenery.

◄ ❸ DECORATIVE GRAVEL

This gold-colored aquarium gravel is used to form a "path" effect through the rocks, adding a rough texture to the base of the tank. You will need about 1lb (500g) in total. Wash well before use to remove any dust.

► ❹ SILICA SAND

Golden silica sand provides a realistic desert effect. The bases of the cacti and rocks can be easily buried in it. As the fish swim about the tank, small sand dunes will quickly form. For a 3 in (7.5cm) layer in a medium-sized tank, you'll need about 45lb (20kg).

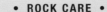

ALTERNATIVE FISH

DWARF RAINBOW FISH

Bright and colorful, these hardy, shoaling fish are relatively easy to keep. They have attractive markings, with red fins and a slight metallic finish to the scales. Use 20 fish for a medium-sized tank.

GREEN SWORDTAIL

A friendly community fish, the Green Swordtail looks striking against the cactus. Active fish, they will dart happily around the tank. Use 20 fish for a medium-sized tank.

ADD TO THE LOOK

A colored background will really help to emphasize the scenery in this tank. For a blue effect, cut a piece of dark blue acrylic sheeting or card to the same length and height as the tank. Secure to the outside back wall with adhesive tape.

zen
GARDEN

A peaceful and serene tank, the Zen garden is a place for contemplation or escapism. This Oriental-style aquarium is inspired by the beauty of Zen thinking, and brings a touch of calming energy.

This tank allows you to create a deep feeling of serenity and stimulation at the same time. The visual interest of the bamboos and delicate layering of the rocks contrast effectively with the smoothness of the sand and plants. Use this tank to bring tranquillity into your home.

THE CAST

SILVER MONO
Silver Monos are very attractive fish, with silver sides and yellow fins. Gliding elegantly through your Zen garden tank, Silver Monos look most effective in shoals of 15 or more.

• FISH CARE •
As Silver Monos are brackish fish, you will need to add 1 teaspoon (5ml) of aquarium salt for every gallon (4.5 liters) of water.

ALTERNATIVE FISH

POLKA DOT MOLLY
Polka Dot Mollies are live-breeders, with black and white colorings and an attractive bulbous body shape. Friendly and sociable, Polka Dot Mollies are a good addition to any community tank. They are best kept together in male–female combinations, and groups of 4 or more.

THE SCENERY

◀ ❶ BAMBOO

Select 3 widths of bamboo, ranging from ¼ in (0.5cm) to 3 in (7.5cm) wide. Saw 2 pieces of the widest bamboo at a 45-degree angle to just within the water height of the tank. Cut a slightly shorter piece from the widest bamboo to stand in front. Still cutting at an angle, saw about 7 pieces of the middle width to create the undulating wall around the widest pieces. Cut up to 20 pieces of the narrowest width to create the second wall. Re-saw the end of each piece at a 90-degree angle to create a level base. Starting at the right-hand corner of the tank, rehearse the arrangement of the bamboo to check the height of each piece. Re-cut the pieces if necessary, then smooth the edges with sandpaper. To stop the bamboo floating, drill a hole up into the base of each piece to let in the water. Soak the bamboo in water for at least 3 days to remove any sap.

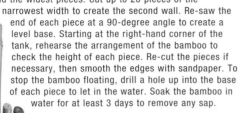

◀ ❷ STRIPED ROCKS

Two smooth, striped rocks, of differing size, are placed on the the left-hand side of the aquarium. The larger ones should be about one-third the length of the aquarium. The smaller stone should be about one-quarter the length of the aquarium.

▲ ❸ WHITE AQUARIUM SAND

Smooth and pale, white aquarium sand provides a peaceful and tranquil base for the tank. For a 3 in (7.5cm) layer in a medium-sized aquarium, you will need about 33lb (15kg) of sand. As the sand is fine, you will also need a piece of aquarium gauze to stop the filtration system from clogging up.

▼ ❹ APONOGETON UNDULATUS

This splendid plant, with ruffled leaves, grows from a rhizome rather than regular roots. You'll need just 1 or 2 plants to place behind the stones.

▼ ❺ FOUNTAIN PLANT

Use 2 or 3 fountain plants, depending on size. They provide detail to the front-right of the tank and set off the bamboo wall.

STAGE SET-UP

Following the rehearsed position, glue the pieces of bamboo to the base of the tank with aquarium silicone adhesive to create the walled display. Carefully add the sand to form the base. Position the larger rock on the left-hand side of the tank, leaving a gap behind for the plants. Place the smaller rock in the center of the tank. Plant the Aponogeton behind the rocks and the Fountain Plant on the far right side. After filling the tank with water, rake the sand with your fingers or a piece of bamboo to create circular lines around the stones.

ADD TO THE LOOK

BLUE ACARA

The Blue Acara is a large, attractive fish with blue stripes on its face and sides. Keep this fish on its own as it is extremely aggressive and fast-moving.

DWARF GOURAMI

Dwarf Gouramis are graceful and elegant fish. The males of these larger Gouramis have red and blue stripes on their sides, and court a female by following her placidly around the tank for hours. Keep these fish together in male–female pairs.

There are plenty of other fish who would enjoy this tank—choose from Guppies, Black Mollies, and Swordfish. Red-clawed Thai Crabs also look great against the sand, though they will obviously disrupt the raked sand.

buried
TREASURE

With its historical theme and simple props, this tank could be straight from an ancient shipwreck or the lost city of Atlantis. It is the perfect design for anyone who loves the romance of the ocean and the mysteries of the ancient world.

The neutrality of terra-cotta and sand will complement the creamy tones chosen in many of today's family homes. Visually harking back to ancient civilizations, this is an easily maintained but effective tank, providing not only shelter and interest for its inhabitants, but also a dramatic display for the viewer.

THE CAST

NEON BLUE DWARF GOURAMI
These graceful Dwarf Gouramis are perfect for keeping in such a tank, as the strong metallic blue stands out magnificently against the orange reds of the terra-cotta. You will need 15 to 20 fish.

RED-CLAWED THAI CRABS
Exciting and active crustaceans, Red-Clawed Thai Crabs are a welcome addition to the aquarium. Crabs are not only fascinating to watch, but they will keep the floor of the tank free from debris. Use a small group of 3 or 4 crabs, making sure they are the same size to avoid territorial battles.

ALTERNATIVE FISH

CARDINAL TETRA
The Cardinal Tetra's strong hues of fluorescent blue-green and bright red will stand out well against the sand and terra-cotta color. If kept in a shoal, these fish will create a dazzling display as well as being fascinating to watch as they dart in and out of the small pots. Use in addition to, or as an alternative to, the Gouramis.

THE SCENERY

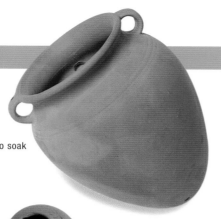

▶ ❶ TERRA-COTTA URN

A single, flat-sided terra-cotta urn, of the kind designed to hang against a garden wall, forms the centerpiece of this tank. Ideally, it should be about one-quarter or one-third the length of the tank. Be sure to soak and wash the urn well before use.

◀ ❷ ROUND TERRA-COTTA POTS

These rustic-looking pots make perfect hiding places for the fish and add an extra sense of antiquity to the tank. For a medium-sized tank, you will need to use 5 pots of various sizes. Wash well before use.

◀ ❸ PEARL-EFFECT BEADS

Plastic, pearl-effect beads create the illusion of wealth that we often associate with the buried treasure. Select a dozen or so beads, measuring ½–1½ in (1–3.75cm) in diameter.

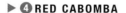

▶ ❹ RED CABOMBA

The rich purple and reds in the Red Cabomba's leaves bring out the color in the pots. The plant adds a soft, flowing dimension to the tank. You will need 5 or 6 plants, depending on size.

STAGE SET-UP

Place the urn flat-side down on the sand. Build up a little sand under the front to raise it slightly. Fill with 1 in (2.5cm) sand to give a settled effect. Place a round terra-cotta pot to the side of the urn to create a sense of scale. Leaving a space at the back for the Cabomba plant, build up the remaining pots on the other side of the tank, varying the angle to add height. Carefully plant the Cabomba behind the round pots. Scatter the beads around the edges of the pots and urn.

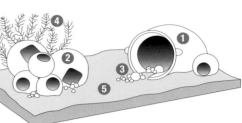

▼ ❺ SILICA SAND

The warm color of golden sand complements the terra-cotta, as well as creating a great seabed effect. It is also easier to position the pots in sand than in gravel. For a 3 in (7.5cm) layer in a medium-sized tank, you will need about 45lb (20kg).

FIREMOUTH

Firemouths enjoy using small spaces such as the terra-cotta pots as a hideaway and lookout. These fish have attractive blue-fringed fins and a red throat section which gently glows during the breeding season, when males provide entertainment with their active rivalry. Although safe with other Cichlids and large fish, Cichlids will eat smaller fish so do not put them with the Gouramis or Tetras.

• FISH CARE •

As crabs like to climb, and may fall onto the floor and dry out, it is important that the aquarium is well secured to prevent them from escaping. Tape up any holes in the tank's lid that could be an escape route. Keep a large piece of glass secured over the air pump pipes so the crabs cannot get a grip and climb out.

morning
MIST

Peaceful and elegant, this aquarium creates the illusion of rolling hills in the first light of a new day, using the simplest of man-made materials— acrylic sheeting and glass pebbles.

Using layers of acrylic sheeting in a variety of bluey tones, this tank allows you to create an original and easy-to-maintain environment. The fish look stunning silhouetted against the light which shines through the acrylic sheets, and their outline is gently blurred as they swim between the vertical layers.

THE CAST

BLACK GUPPY
The Black Guppy contrasts most dramatically with the colors and flowing edges of the contoured acrylic sheets. Their darkness shows up strongly as they glide between the different layers. Use 30 to 40 fish for a medium-sized tank. If using both males and females, be aware that the females will fall pregnant after a few weeks and most of the young fry will be eaten by the adult fish.

ALTERNATIVE FISH

BLACK WIDOW
The Black Widow has a silver body with 3 black stripes down the side. The fish also has a black rear half, which stands out against the background of the tank. This fish can be used in addition to the Black Guppy or as an alternative.

BLACK ANGELFISH
Conspicuous against the pale blues, Black Angelfish will glide elegantly around this sophisticated and serene aquarium. Do not use this fish with the Black Guppy or Black Widow as it is too aggressive.

THE SCENERY

◄ ❶ ACRYLIC SHEETING

You will need 6 pieces of thin acrylic sheeting—2 of each color—to fit the height and length of the inside of the tank. The darkest piece is used for the background and the remaining pieces are cut to create the "hills," which are positioned to allow the fish to swim between them.

To create the "hills," draw out 5 templates on separate sheets of tracing paper. Overlay the sheets to check the shapes work together and adjust if necessary. Lay each template over an acrylic sheet and tape down with low-tack tape to secure. Working on a cutting board, cut through the template with a craft knife to score the acrylic. Continue cutting until you have cut the acrylic all the way through. Smooth the cut edges with wet-dry sandpaper if necessary.

STAGE SET-UP

For the background, take the darkest sheet of acrylic and run a line of aquarium silicone adhesive along the edge. Stick firmly to the inside back wall of the tank.

Work out the intended position of the 5 "hills" and mark with a piece of low-tack tape on the outside of the tank.

Starting from the back, apply a line of aquarium silicone adhesive along the base of the tank where the first "hill" will be positioned. Press the base of the acrylic into the adhesive. Use a wet finger to smooth the edges of the adhesive onto the acrylic and tank base. Then, apply a line of adhesive to the back of the acrylic where it meets the side of the tank. Again, run a wet finger along the acrylic and tank wall to smooth the join, pressing firmly and taking care that the adhesive doesn't show on the front of the acrylic. Allow the adhesive to set.

Assemble the remaining "hills" in the same way, allowing each one to dry in turn. When all the "hills" are in position, remove the tape from the outside of the tank and leave for at least 2 days to allow the adhesive to set completely. Finally, add the glass pebbles between the layers to create the base.

► ❷ GLASS PEBBLES

Measuring about ½ in (1cm) in diameter, pale-blue and pale-green glass pebbles complement the colored acrylic landscape. For a 3 in (7.5cm) layer in a medium-sized tank, you will need about 16lb (7kg) each of the blue and green pebbles. Alternatively, mix a smaller quantity of glass pebbles with your regular aquarium flooring to give a subtler effect.

ADD TO THE LOOK

• FISH CARE •

As there are no plants in this tank to create oxygen, make sure your filtration system is working well. Make sure the "hills" are well secured to the floor of the tank and there is enough room between them to allow the fish to swim freely.

You can use other colors of acrylic sheeting to create different moods: reds, oranges, and yellows will give you the "feel" of Arizona or the Australian outback, while greens may suggest the green hillsides of Kentucky. Grays and blues can be used to create an urban style, especially if you cut the pieces into the angular shapes of a modern skyline.

opaque
PLANET

Looking like a set from a cult science-fiction film, this tank uses everyday objects in an unusual way to create a fascinating and stylish aquarium that will surprise and intrigue guests.

This aquarium provides a thrillingly futuristic display, while creating an enjoyable and comfortable space for your fish to explore. Ordinary light bulbs and lamp shades provide the main design focus of this cool-looking tank. Red and black Bubble-Eye Fantails complement the look to create an out-of-this-world centerpiece, perfect for your new living room, vestibule, or even your bedroom.

THE CAST

RED AND BLACK BUBBLE-EYE FANTAIL
These fancy, graceful Goldfish will glide slowly around their light fantastic habitat with interest. With bulbous bodies and bubbles forming underneath their eyes, Bubble-Eye Fantails help enhance the "brave new world" feel of this tank. As these are cold water fish, it is not necessary to provide a heater for them. Use 10 black fish and 5 red ones for a medium-sized tank.

ALTERNATIVE FISH

• FISH CARE •
Bubble-Eyes can be prone to eye damage because their eyes protrude so prominently. Take extra care that there is nothing jagged in the tank that may tear their delicate eye sacs. Even though neither Bubble-Eyes nor Moors require a water heater, it is important to provide an air pump so that the water is oxygenated sufficiently.

THE SCENERY

▶ ① OPAQUE LIGHT BULBS

You will need 8 bulbs of various sizes. To prevent rust from polluting the water, coat the metal base of each bulb with yacht varnish or aquarium silicone adhesive and leave to dry for at least 2 days. To vary the height of the smaller bulbs, you will also need large stones, about 2 in (5cm) thick, to which the bulbs will be stuck with aquarium silicone adhesive.

▶ ④ OPAQUE GLASS PEBBLES

These iridescent pebbles continue the globular effect of the tank and add a shiny feel to the base of the aquarium. For a 3 in (7.5cm) layer in a medium-sized tank you will need about 33lb (15kg) in total.

◀ ② OPAQUE LAMP SHADES

Use 2 opaque glass lamp shades, measuring approximately one-eighth the size of the tank.

▶ ③ PEARL-EFFECT PLANTS

For further decorative effect, use 2 plastic pearl-effect plants. Even though they are not organic, the plants will still provide valuable extra shelter for your fish as well as adding height to your design.

STAGE SET-UP

Firstly, rehearse the position of the bulbs in the tank. Decide which of the smaller bulbs should be raised and select a suitable stone to which these bulbs will be stuck. Squeeze a mound of aquarium silicone adhesive to each stone and push the bulb into it. Use a wet finger to make sure the metal base is completely coated in adhesive. Leave to dry for 2 days, then place in the tank. Use aquarium silicone adhesive to fix the remaining bulbs to the base of the tank in the same way. Add the glass pebbles around the bulbs, taking care to cover the stones and bulb bases. Position 1 lamp shade in the left-hand corner and 1 off-center to the right. Position the plants behind the lamp shades.

ADD TO THE LOOK

TELESCOPE-EYE FANTAIL

The standard Telescope-Eye Fantail is an instantly recognizable strain and makes a suitable replacement for, or addition to, the Bubble-Eye Fantail. Each eye is surrounded by a fluid-filled sac, and this wobbles about as the fish swims. Body colors varies, but is usually metallic red or orange.

BLACK MOOR

Not unlike the Telescope-Eye Fantail, the Black Moor has a bulbous body and large eyes, though these are not as pronounced as those of their relatives. Moors also have a distinctive fantail and will move sedately around the tank. A slightly hardier cold water fish than the Telescope-Eye Fantail, they could be an appropriate choice for a child's version of this tank. Use 20 fish for a medium-sized tank.

You could include 4 or 5 more bulbs and build the tank up at the back. This will create small crevices for your fish to rest in. You will need to stick any extra bulbs in place with aquarium silicone adhesive to prevent them from floating away. If you'd like a background color, cut a piece of red paper to the length and height of your tank. Using aquarium silicone adhesive, stick it firmly to the inside or outside back wall of your tank.

glass HOUSE

Everything about this tank is totally transparent. By using everyday materials, you can create an aquarium that is as see-through as the water itself, leaving your fish to be the stars of the show.

▲ ❶ GLASS VASES AND TUMBLERS

These vases and tumblers in different heights and widths create a dramatic display in this tank and give your fish smooth items to swim between and around. You will need 1 vase that is as tall as the tank and 3 vases that are three-quarters the height of the tank. Select 5 drinking tumblers of various sizes.

To emphasize the transparent theme already provided by the clear glass of the tank itself, and the water that fills it, use a selection of clear glass jars, tumblers, and rods in this aquarium. This clever design allows you to see your fish at all times, yet provides them with adequate shade so that they feel at home too.

▼ ❷ GLASS BEADS

Glass beads create a transparent look on the base of your tank. Glass beads are available from florists, craft stores, and glass manufacturers. For a 3 in (7.5cm) layer in a medium-sized tank, you will need about 33lb (15kg).

▶ ❸ GLASS RODS

When the fish swim behind these simple glass rods, the refraction of light will create stunning effects. The rods are available from lab suppliers and craft stores. You will need 6 rods that are as tall as the tank and 12 rods that are half the height of the tank.

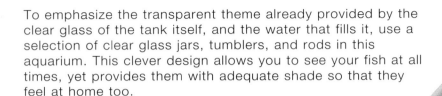

THE SCENERY

STAGE SET-UP

Place the largest vase in the left-hand back corner of the tank. Surround with 2 more vases and the tumblers. Position the last vase in the right-hand corner of the tank, and surround with the glass rods to form 2 semi-circular "fences." To secure the rods, squeeze a mound of aquarium silicone adhesive onto the tank base for each rod, starting at the back. Gently push the rods into the adhesive. Hold each one in place until it feels secure. Leave to set for 2 days. Fill the base carefully with the glass pebbles, then gently pour more glass beads into the tumblers and vases to the same level.

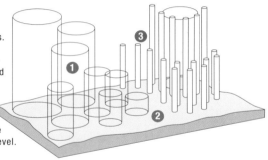

THE CAST

SPOTTED SCAT

The Spotted Scat is covered in leopard-like spots and has an attractive hue to its scales. These medium-sized fish are active and lively, darting between the glassware in your tank to provide plenty of visual interest. As they move between the glass objects in your tank, the light refracts to create endless interesting shapes. Use 30 fish for a medium-sized tank.

ALTERNATIVE FISH

BLUE PANGASSIUS
This inquisitive catfish needs plenty of space to roam the lower levels of the tank. Use up to 10 fish in a medium-sized tank.

• FISH CARE •
Fish need sleep too, so remember to turn off the tank light for a reasonable amount of time. In this way your fish can escape the glare generated by this transparent tank which only has a limited amount of shade. Ensure the filtration system is strong as there are no plants to provide extra oxygen output.

GLASS CATFISH
Glass Catfish are rather nervous fish, best kept in shoals of 6 or more. Almost completely see-through, Glass Catfish, or Ghost Catfish, as they are sometimes known, are perfect for this kind of tank. Use 10 fish for a medium-sized tank.

GLOWLIGHT TETRA
Small and transparent, apart from a bright orange stripe running along their middle, Glowlight Tetras are most attractive kept in shoals of 4 or more. Use 20 fish for a medium-sized tank.

HEAD-AND-TAIL-LIGHT TETRA
Almost transparent, Head-and-Tail-Light Tetras are lively little fish. They are best kept in small groups—use no more than 20 in a medium-sized tank.

plastic
PLAYGROUND

Perfect for a household with young children, or for adults who prefer a funky, modern look, this themed, plastic playground tank is bright and cheerful, and provides the ideal opportunity for endless aquatic aerobics performed by vividly colored Mollies.

The original use of a selection of rodent runs and caged bird toys creates an eye-catching, colorful, and fun aquarium that your fish will enjoy—while the whole family will find it thrilling to watch. With a range of differently sized tubes for your fish to swim along, and rings and hoops for them to dart through, this is the ultimate activity center for lively fish, such as Balloon Mollies.

THE CAST

ASSORTED HI-FIN BALLOON MOLLY
Balloon Mollies are colorful fish with a wonderfully bulbous body shape that fits in perfectly with this fun primary-colored tank. Use 16 to 18 fish for a medium-sized tank.

ALTERNATIVE FISH

ASSORTED PLATY
Much like Mollies, colorful Platies are adventurous, and happy to swim through the tubes and rings in this tank. You will need 18 to 20 fish for a medium-sized tank.

THE SCENERY

▼ ⑤ RED AQUARIUM GRAVEL
Red aquarium gravel adds a really bright base to this tank and provides an anchor for the hoops and ladder. Wash it well before use, as the excess dye could cloud the water. For a 3 in (7.5cm) layer in a medium-sized tank, you will need about 33lb (15kg).

◀ ① PLASTIC TUBES
Hamster or rodent housing is used to great effect in this tank. Select a variety of curved tubes and connectors in different colors, and practice combining them into a curvy X-shape using the manufacturer's instructions. You may need to use aquarium silicone adhesive to secure the pieces when you create the final arrangement.

▼ ② PLASTIC HOOPS
Linked plastic hoops, most commonly used in bird cages, add extra visual interest to the tank and provide plenty of fun for the fish. Use 2 sizes of hoops, each with 5 rings. Stand the largest hoops upright in the gravel. Suspend the smaller hoops from glass rods placed across the top of the tank.

▼ ③ GLASS RODS
To hang the plastic hoops, you will need 2 to 4 glass rods that are long enough to lie across the top of the tank. If necessary, secure into position with silicone adhesive.

▲ ④ PLASTIC LADDER
You will need 1 plastic parrot or bird ladder that is slightly taller than the tank. Remove any metal or plastic attachments from the end of the ladder before use.

STAGE SET-UP
Lay the gravel base. Fix the hamster tubes into your desired shape and secure together with aquarium silicone adhesive. Leave to dry for 2 days. Place the construction in the tank. Rest the ladder against the back of the tank running between the tubes on the right. Bury the larger plastic hoops in the gravel toward the back of the tank on the left. Suspend the smaller hoops from glass rods so they hang in the water.

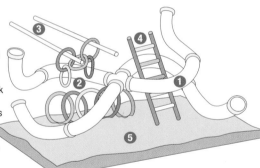
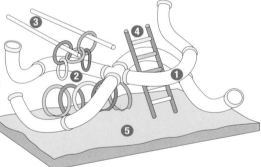

ADD TO THE LOOK

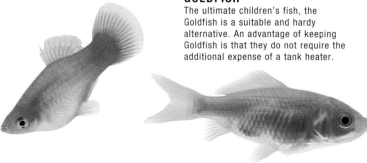

GOLDFISH
The ultimate children's fish, the Goldfish is a suitable and hardy alternative. An advantage of keeping Goldfish is that they do not require the additional expense of a tank heater.

• FISH CARE •
Look over all the tubes, hoops and ladders to ensure that there are no sharp edges or pieces of plastic sticking out, on which your fish could damage their scales or fins. Also make sure that the hoops you use are large enough for your biggest fish to swim through with comfort and ease.

You may want to add to the colorful theme of the tank by including a selection of neon-colored plastic plants or using a mix-and-match range of different-colored gravel.

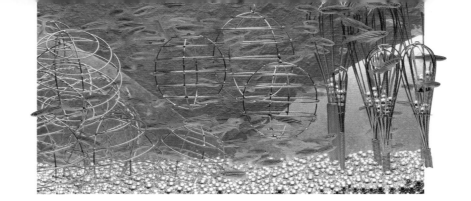

metallic
LANDSCAPE

A futuristic airy-looking aquarium filled with minute, fast-moving colorful fish, to provide a fascinating display full of shapes to interest your fish, and keep you absorbed for hours.

Shiny and bright, this metallic tank is modern and exciting, but still has plenty of places for your fish to play, hide, and display themselves at their best. Everyday kitchen utensils and Christmas ornaments are cleverly combined to create a shimmering, almost iridescent aquarium that can take pride of place in your living room or even your kitchen or bathroom.

THE CAST

LONG-FINNED ZEBRA DANIO
The lively and playful Long-Finned Zebra Danio will dart around this tank for hours as it amuses itself by gliding through the gaps in your decorations. This elegant variety of Danio, with its elongated fins, creates a more fluid feeling of movement than its short-finned cousins. Use 100 fish in a medium-sized tank.

ALTERNATIVE FISH

CARDINAL TETRA
Small, shoaling fish, Cardinal Tetras sport striking red, blue, and silver stripes that show up superbly against this dramatic metallic backdrop. Use 50 fish in a medium-sized tank.

CHERRY BARB
Cherry Barbs are small, bright red fish which will dart around your aquarium happily. Use 150 fish in a medium-sized tank.

THE SCENERY

◀ **①** METALLIC BAUBLES

Metallic baubles, such as those sold as Christmas decorations, make ideal props for this tank. Ideally, select baubles that are made of stainless steel. Alternatively, coat completely with non-toxic acrylic sealant before use, taking care to sand off any sharp edges beforehand. You will need 9 baubles of varying sizes—the largest should be no more than one-quarter the size of the tank and the smallest should about one-eighth the size of the tank.

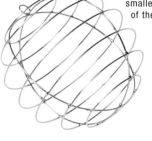

▶ **③** SILVER BEADS

Use metallic beads or ball bearings to create the base of the tank. For a 3 in (7.5cm) layer in a medium-sized tank, you will need about 33lb (15kg) of beads or balls. Alternatively, use a smaller quantity and place over a layer of glass pebbles.

▼ **④** BALLOON WHISKS

Use 8 to 10 stainless steel balloon whisks of various sizes to create "trees" for this tank. Before use, remove any hooks from the base of the whisks with metal cutters, then sand the cut edges until smooth.

◀ **②** METAL SHEETING

For the "hills," you will need a piece of metal sheeting, such as tin or steel, measuring a little larger than the tank. Draw 2 "hills" on the metal with a felt-tip pen, measuring two-thirds the tank height and just over half the length. Depending on the thickness of the sheeting, use metal cutters or a metal saw to cut out the "hill" shapes. Sand the cut edges gently. Dab a little aquarium silicone adhesive along the "hill" edges, then stick to the outside back wall of the tank. Secure with low-tack tape until dry.

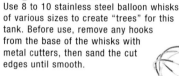

◀ **⑤** GLASS RODS

You will need about 3 to 4 glass rods from which to suspend the metallic baubles.

STAGE SET-UP

Rehearse the position of the whisks on the right-hand side of the tank. Starting at the back, squeeze mounds of aquarium silicone adhesive onto the tank base. Push the base of each whisk into the adhesive and hold until secure. Leave for 2 days, or until set. Add the beads to create the base. Place 1 medium-sized bauble in front of the whisks, and place the largest bauble at the back left-hand corner. Pile 5 baubles on and around it, securing with aquarium silicone adhesive if necessary. Suspend the remaining baubles on nylon thread from glass rods resting across the tank.

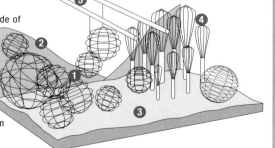

ADD TO THE LOOK

For a background color to highlight the stunning props in this tank, cut a sheet of hand-made paper to the same height and length as the tank. Use invisible tape to secure it to the back wall, behind the metallic "hills."

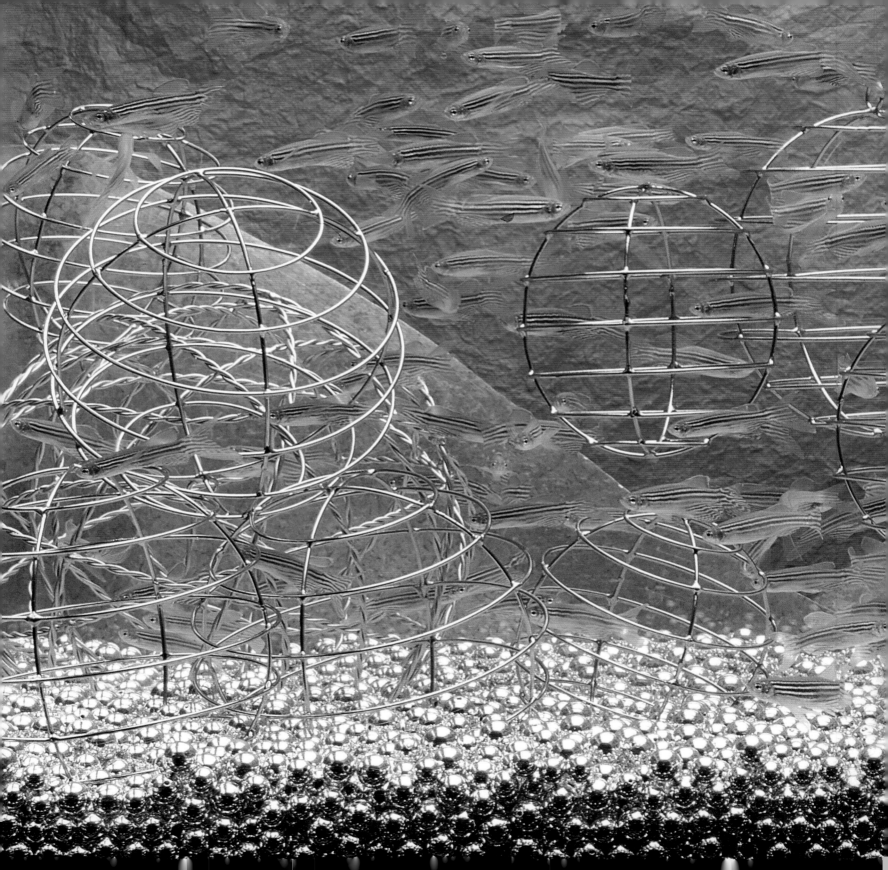

winter
WONDERLAND

In the middle of winter, there is nothing like Christmas celebrations to put everyone in a good mood. This festive tank is perfect for this time of year.

This design shows just what you can achieve with Christmas decorations, glass pebbles, and the desire to create something truly original! To make the "plants," lengths of plastic garland are first buried in the glass bead floor, then polystyrene balls are stuck to the garland to help it float.

Plastic snowflakes are suspended from glass rods balanced over the top of the tank using lengths of nylon thread. The brightly colored fish will be as happy as Santa's little helpers as they dart around their glittering new home.

THE CAST

NEON ROSY BARB
The metallic finish on the scales of the Neon Rosy Barb complements the decorations in this aquarium perfectly.
Being reasonably sized fish, they do not get overshadowed by the hanging snowflakes, and they can swim gracefully around the tank. These colorful gold and silver fish will show a lively interest in their surroundings, and are perfectly happy in this aquarium. Use about 25 fish.

ALTERNATIVE FISH

RED EYE TETRA
Medium-sized silver fish, Red Eye Tetras have bright red eyes, and a black stripe by the base of the tail. They are happiest in large groups, though tend to pick on smaller fish if kept in groups as part of a community tank. However, in a solitary shoal, they make a dazzling and effective alternative to Neon Rosy Barbs, and will live peacefully in each other's company.

CONGO TETRA
With its large scales, which reflect changing colors in a similar way to opal gemstones, the Congo Tetra is a beautiful alternative to the Neon Rosy Barb. Its black, middle tail rays are extended into a ragged edge, and the male has an elongated dorsal and anal fin. Congo Tetras do very well in shoals and are very peaceful towards other fish.

THE SCENERY

◀ ❶ PLASTIC SNOWFLAKES

Plastic snowflake decorations are widely available at Christmas. You will need about 20, measuring 1 in to 3 in (2.5cm to 7.5cm) in diameter. Choose a variety of sizes in both clear and opaque plastic. Before use, smooth the edges with wet-dry sandpaper and clean well. The snowflakes will spin slowly in the current of the filtered water. Do not use snowflakes with any kind of adornment or decoration, such as glitter, attached to the surface.

◀ ❷ SILVER GARLAND

You will need about 20 lengths of plain plastic silver garland. This should be cut to various lengths, but no longer than the height of the tank. Stick the strips along a piece of non-toxic adhesive tape, measuring about half the length of the tank. Fold the tape into a fan shape to create the "plant." Use aquarium silicone adhesive to stick polystyrene balls to the top end of some of the strips to make them float. Carefully wrap a piece of aquarium lead strip around the taped end, then bury under the pebbles.

▶ ❸ OPAQUE GLASS PEBBLES

Opaque glass pebbles create the effect of freshly fallen snow, reflecting the light and adding a touch of extra sparkle. Choose pebbles about ½ in (1cm) in diameter; for a 3 in (7.5cm) layer in a medium-sized tank, you will need about 33lb (15kg).

STAGE SET-UP

Position the garland "plant" on the base of the tank, then add the glass pebbles to create the floor. Tie the snowflakes to lengths of nylon thread. Cut the threads to various lengths, but no shorter than half the height of the tank. Tie the snowflakes to the glass rods. Space the hanging snowflakes evenly along the rods. Lay the rods over the tank to suspend the snowflakes, then secure the rods to the tank with a little aquarium silicone adhesive. Untangle the garland if necessary.

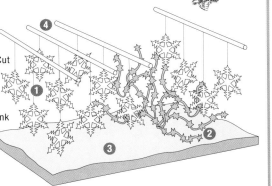

▶ ❹ GLASS RODS

Glass rods are used to suspend the plastic snowflakes. Glass casts less shadow than wood, but you can use strips of wood instead if glass rods are unavailable. You'll need about 4 rods; make sure they are long enough to fit across the shelf which lies inside the tank edge.

ADD TO THE LOOK

ALBINO TIGER BARB

The Albino Tiger Barb is one of the most attractive members of the Barb family, with orangey scales and a pale underside. When used instead of the Neon Rosy Barb in this display, this active shoaling fish, provides plenty of entertainment for the viewers.

• FISH CARE •

As this tank has a minimal amount of shade, turn off the tank light for as long as possible to let the fish rest. Always maintain a strong filtration system, as there are no plants to output oxygen. Refer to pages 12–13 for more information on safety and preparing your tank scenery.

Instead of making the garland "plant," you may prefer to use silver or pearl-effect plastic aquarium plants.

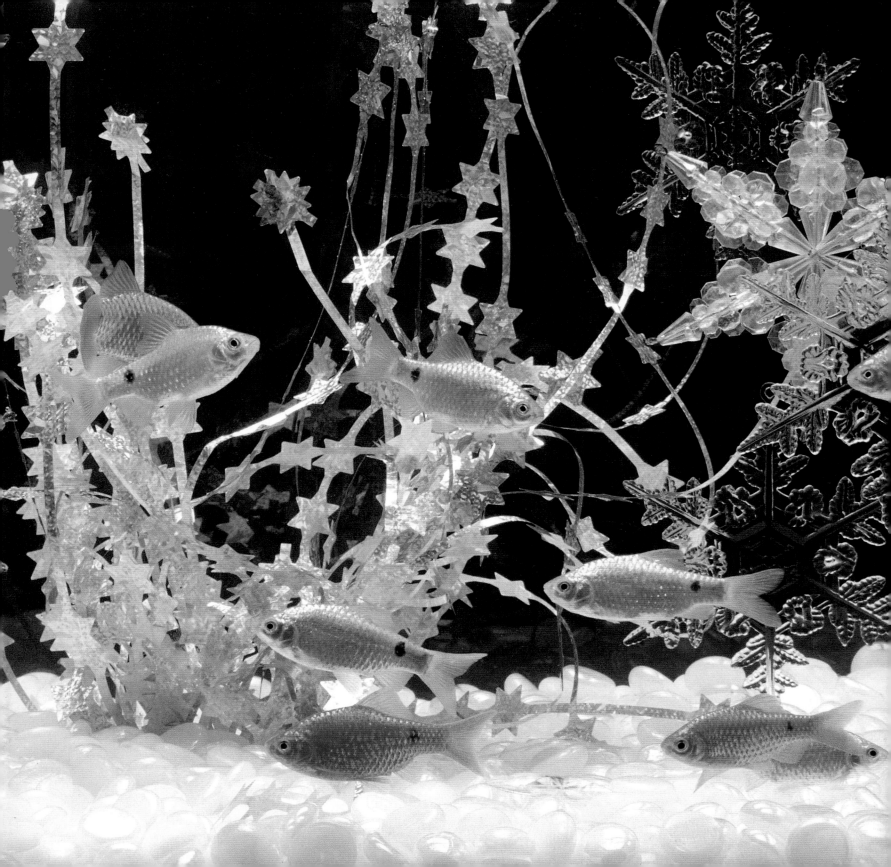

fish directory

Aequidens pulcher
Blue Acara
A pale gray body marked with brown bars distinguishes this cichlid, although it is the metallic blue scale centers that catch the eye. It originates in South America and will grow up to 6 in (15cm) long in a spacious tank. It tolerates most water conditions and prefers the company of its own species.

Arius seemani
Shark Catfish
Originally from Southeast Asia this fish will grow to about 12 in (30cm) long in a large tank. Later in life it is best kept in brackish water to which a teaspoon of aquarium salt has been added, but will cope in fresh water while younger.

Astronotus ocellatus
Red (or Tiger) Oscar
This large, active fish from South America is a voracious eater and grows up to 12 in (30cm) in length: a big tank with plenty of swimming room is required. The Oscar likes to dig, so sand or gravel is a more suitable base for the aquarium.

Balantiocheilus melanopterus
Silver Shark
Also known as the Bala Shark, this large shoaling fish comes from Thailand, where it can reach 16 in (40cm) in length in the wild. Aquarium-reared specimens will be smaller, but owners should be aware of its powerful jumping ability, and keep it in a tightly covered tank. Hardy and mild-tempered, it is not sensitive to water types.

Barbus conchonius var.
Neon Rosy Barb
This active and peaceful aquarium fish is good for beginners. Adult fish may grow to about 4 in (10cm) and, although hardy, do best in medium-hard water. Use sand as a base as the fish tend to burrow.

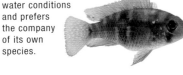

Barbus nigrofasciatus
Black Ruby Barb
This beautiful fish comes from Sri Lanka and grows to a length of around 2 in (5cm). Very hardy, it can cope with most water types.

Barbus sachsi
Golden Barb
This bright yellow barb, a native of southern China and Vietnam, is sometimes confused with the related Schuberti Barb. It grows to about 3 in (7.5cm) long, and prefers slightly acidic, aged water.

Barbus tetrazona
Tiger Barb
Also known as the Sumatran Barb, an indicator of its Southeast Asian origins, this popular fish has bold and instantly recognizable coloring. It requires plenty of oxygenated, slightly acidic water to thrive, and grows to around 2½ in (6cm) long under aquarium conditions.

Barbus tetrazona var.
Albino Tiger Barb
The albino variant of the Tiger Barb is paler than its striped cousin, but has the same requirements: it should be kept in small shoals with limited vegetation and soft to medium-hard water. Do not put them together with Angelfish; the Barbs tend to nip their fins.

Barbus tetrazona var.
Green Tiger Barb
An aquarium-bred variant with blotches of dark color replacing the tiger stripes, this can be a more aggressive shoaling species. Keep separate from Angelfish, as noted previously.

Barbus titteya
Cherry Barb
This barb comes from Sri Lanka and grows to just under 2 in (5cm) long. Cherry Barbs are active shoaling fish and can be kept in groups of 10 or more. They enjoy subdued lighting and marginal vegetation in a tank.

Botia macracantha
Clown Loach
Perhaps the most popular member of the genus *Botia*, this fish can grow to around 12 in (30cm) in length, but seldom gets that big in captivity. It has an unusual habit of swimming in shoals with other striped fish, especially with Tiger Barbs.

Brachydanio rerio
Zebra Danio
Bright blue or purple horizontal stripes on a base of silver or gold identify the species type of this active little fish from India's east coast.

Brachydanio rerio var.
Long-Finned Zebra Danio
This popular long-finned variant of the Zebra Danio, a river fish from India and Bangladesh, grows to around 2 in (5cm) long. A hardy specimen, it is best kept in groups of six or more, when it will shoal at the front of the aquarium.

Carassius auratus
Goldfish
The common goldfish originated in China and other parts of eastern Asia and was greenish bronze in color. With selective breeding there are now many color variations but the most common is a vibrant orange. The goldfish is extremely hardy and can tolerate many different types of water conditions— goldfish are cold-blooded and do not need to be kept in heated water. The fish can grow up to 20 in (50cm) long if kept in a very large tank or pond. However, they can be added to a tropical aquarium as long as the other fish in the tank are sufficiently large.

Carassius auratus var.
Black Moor
This graceful goldfish variation is noted for its deep black coloring and protruding eyes. As a cold water Cyprinid, this fish requires more swimming space than tropical freshwater fish and a shady position for the tank.

Carassius auratus var.
Bubble-Eye Fantail
This extraordinary-looking goldfish has distinctive fluid-filled sacs surrounding each eye, which wobble as the fish swims. It is best kept with its own kind.

Carassius auratus var.
Telescope-Eye Fantail
Instantly recognizable with its telescopic eyes and double caudal fin, this is one of a number of twin-tailed strains cultivated in Japan and increasingly popular in aquariums.

Cheirodon axelrodi
Cardinal Tetra

A striking little fish from the Rio Negro in Brazil, the Cardinal Tetra grows to about 1½ in (3cm) long. It enjoys a shoal lifestyle and subdued lighting, and prefers "black water," which is achieved by filtering soft, acidic water through peat.

Colisa chuna
Honey Gourami

This striking Gourami is initially quite shy and best kept in a species tank. It appears to prefer slightly acidic water.

Colisa lalia
Dwarf Gourami

This very attractive Gourami from India and Bangladesh has bright red and blue coloration in the male. A small and peaceful fish, it grows up to about 2 in (5cm) in length. It is hardy and will thrive in a community aquarium.

Colisia lalia var.
Neon Blue Dwarf Gourami

A blue strain of the Dwarf Gourami from India, this fish prefers soft, slightly acidic water in the aquarium.

Corydoras arcuatus
Arched Catfish

With a prominent band of color running along its back, the Arched Catfish is an impressive addition to any tank. To protect its delicate barbels, place in a tank with a soft, sandy substrate, rather than coarse gravel. Do not keep in overly acidic water.

Corydoras haraldschultzi
Harald Shultz's Cory

Found in the sandy streams of the Amazon, this catfish enjoys a well-planted tank with open areas of soft sand. It will grow up to 3 in (7.5cm) long.

Cyphotilapia frontosa
Frontosa

Also known as the Deep-Water Cichlid, this boldly striped fish comes from the rocky lakes of East Africa, where it can reach 12 in to 16 in (30cm to 40cm) in length. Its natural habitat means that it needs hard, alkaline water.

Gymnocorymbus ternetzi
Black Widow

Also known as the Black Tetra, this smoky gray fish is particularly attractive when young. Growing to around 2½ in (6cm) long, it is a good all-rounder, tolerant of others, and easy to breed in a well-planted aquarium.

Hasemania nana
Silver-Tipped Tetra

This tetra comes from the Amazon rain forest and therefore thrives best in soft, acidic water which should be kept slightly warmer than normal. This stunning little fish grows to around 2 in (5cm) long.

Helostoma temmincki var.
Pink Kissing Gourami

The wild form of this colored variant can reach 12 in (30cm) long in its native Malaysia and Thailand, but in the tank it will rarely exceed 6 in (15cm). It is best kept in soft, acidic water.

Hemigrammus erythrozonus
Glowlight Tetra

One of the most popular and beautiful of tetras, this fish hails from Guyana and grows to 1½ in (4cm) in length. It thrives in soft, slightly acidic water and prefers patches of dense vegetation, as well as plenty of open water near the bottom of the tank.

Hemigrammus ocellifer
Head-and-Tail-Light Tetra

Also known as the Beacon Fish, this tiny tetra originates in the Amazon region. It can be kept in most types of water and enjoys a community tank.

Herichthys meeki
Firemouth

This cichlid inhabits streams and rivers in Yucatan, Mexico and Guatemala. It usually grows to 6 in (15cm), and is distinguished by its fiery red chest. Best kept in a well planted tank with other large fish as it can be aggressive.

Hyphessobrycon pulchripinnis
Lemon Tetra

From the Amazon region, this yellow tetra has beautiful, subtle coloration. It grows to around 2 in (5cm) long, and prefers neutral to slightly acidic water.

Hyphessobrycon serpae
Serpae Tetra

This characin from South America grows to 2 in (5cm) in the aquarium. Blood-red fading to pale, it is identified by the dark, comma-shaped spot on the shoulder. It is an easy fish to keep, preferring soft water, and is not difficult to breed, making it an ideal beginner's specimen.

Kryptopterus bicirrhis
Glass Catfish

This striking fish from Southeast Asia is completely transparent, its backbone and internal organs clearly visible through its scaleless skin. Active during the daylight hours, it is best kept in numbers.

Labeo erythrurus
Red-Finned Shark

This fish from Thailand grows up to 5 in (12.5cm) long. It requires soft, acidic water and prefers the bottom layers of the tank.

Melanotaenia maccullochi
Dwarf Rainbow Fish

The Dwarf Rainbow Fish is an active shoaling fish from northern Australia. It can grow to about 3 in (7.5cm) long. This is a hardy fish and prefers hard, alkaline water.

Microgeophagus ramirezi
Ram

This iridescent cichlid requires slightly acidic water in a tank with plenty of shelter. It grows up to 2 in (5cm) long and does well in a community tank with similarly sized fish.

Microgeophagus ramirezi var.
Gold Ram

This is an aquarium-bred color form of the wild Ram that was previously placed in the genus *Papiliochromis*, now reclassified as *Microgeophagus*. It grows up to 2 in (5cm) long and prefers slightly acidic water in a community aquarium.

Moenkhausia sanctae-filomenae
Red Eye Tetra
This large and attractive tetra comes from South America. It seems to do best in slightly hard, alkaline water, is easy to keep, and grows up to around 2½ in (6cm) long.

Monodactylus argenteus
Silver Mono
This attractive shoaling fish from Southeast Asia is also known as a Fingerfish, Silver Finger, or Malay Angel. It can grow up to 8 in (20cm) long and swims in mid-water. Usually found in estuaries in the wild, it needs brackish water—add a teaspoon of aquarium salt per gallon to the tank.

Nematobrycon palmeri var.
Purple Emperor Tetra
This colorful form of the Emperor Tetra comes from Colombia and grows to just under 3 in (7.5cm) in length. It is a reasonably hardy fish, eats almost anything, and can be kept in most water conditions. It does well when kept in a shoal of 10 or more.

Pangasius sutchi
Blue Pangassius
These hardy fish can tolerate most types of water conditions. They are very active, and happiest when kept in shoals.

Pangasius sutchi var.
Albino Pangasius
This albino form of the Asian Shark Catfish can grow up to 18 in (45cm) long if placed in a large, sparsely populated tank. This hardy fish can tolerate most water types and is happiest when kept in shoals.

Paracheirodon innesi
Neon Tetra
Distinguished by the electric blue stripe that runs the length of its body, this is a favorite fish for many aquarium keepers. Originally from the Amazon, it prefers soft, acidic water which has been filtered through peat, and grows to around 1 in (2.5cm) long.

Phenacogrammus interruptus
Congo Tetra
This lovely characin from Zaire has very large, opaline scales. It can grow to nearly 5 in (13cm) in length. Congo Tetras are happiest in soft, acidic, and peat-strained water.

Pimelodella pictus
Angelicus Pimelodella
This distinctive catfish can grow up to 4½ in (11cm). Its sharp dorsal and pectoral spines make it difficult to handle. It prefers slightly acidic water.

Poecilia latipinna
Hi-Fin Balloon Molly
With its huge dorsal fin, this stunning hybrid is available in various colors. It needs plenty of room, and medium-hard, alkaline water.

Poecilia latipinna var.
Polka Dot Molly
This Molly hybrid from Central and South America can grow up to 4 in (10cm) long, with enormous variation in body coloring. It thrives in medium-hard, slightly alkaline water.

Poecilia reticulata var.
Black Guppy
This fish is hardy, easy to breed, and provides an attractive display. There are many variations in color and shape, including round tail, spadetail, speartail, pintail, and fantail variations. The water should be medium-hard (slightly alkaline). Guppies breed easily when kept in mixed-sex groups, but fry should be removed to a separate tank.

Poecilia reticulata var.
Blond Red Guppy
Another variation on the guppy theme, this stunning red fish is a prolific breeder and well suited to a community tank of similarly sized fish. Females are larger and have duller coloration, but are still a worthwhile addition.

Poecilia reticulata var.
Golden Guppy
A colorful variation of one of the best known of all tropical fishes. Bold and active, the hardy guppy is very easy to keep. The water should be slightly alkaline.

Poecilia reticulata var.
Neon Blue Guppy
The original range for this species is northern Brazil to the Caribbean, where it inhabits brackish ponds and books. It is happiest in slightly alkaline, medium-hard water.

Poecilia sphenops var.
Black Molly
Originating in Central America, this fish grows up to 4 in (10cm) long. Males are more intensely colored than females, and both do best when provided with large amounts of vegetable food as part of the diet. Mollies prefer medium-hard water, and some salinity can be tolerated.

Pterophyllum scalare
Common Angelfish
The species type of the common Amazonian Angelfish, these specimens are prized for their elegant shapes and graceful swimming. Like all freshwater Angelfish, both parents take intensive care of their young brood.

Pterophyllum scalare var.
Black Angelfish
This freshwater angelfish has been the subject of selective breeding programs, and is now available in a wide range of color strains. It will grow up to 6 in (15cm) in length and demands plenty of swimming space. Although they prefer soft water, they will tolerate medium-hard water, and enjoy a community tank with similar-sized fish.

Rasbora heteromorpha
Harlequin Rasbora
This popular fish from Southeast Asia is distinguished by the blue-black triangle of color on its flanks. It grows to just under 2 in (5cm) and prefers soft, acidic water, preferably filtered through peat. Harlequins are best kept in groups of six or more.

Rasbora trilineata
Scissortail
Named after the fashion in which it twitches its deeply forked tail when at rest, this Southeast Asian fish may grow to 6 in (15cm), but is usually smaller. It is an active fish, ideal for a community tank.

Red-Clawed Thai Crab
These active crustaceans from Southeast Asia are suitable for many types of tanks. They are happiest in groups of similar-sized Thai Crabs.

Rineloricaria sp.
Whiptailed Catfish
This flattened-looking catfish from Colombia in South America can grow as long as 10 in (25cm) in the wild, but will more likely make half that size in the aquarium. This catfish does best in slightly alkaline water.

Scatophagus argus
Spotted Scat
This fish is found in estuaries and the open sea in the eastern Indian Ocean. As it prefers brackish to fresh water, a teaspoon of aquarium salt per gallon should be added to the tank. Scats can eat huge quantities of food and may even grow to 12 in (30cm) long. Only small specimens are suitable for the home tank.

Serrasalmus nattereri
Red-Bellied Piranha
Notorious for its flesh-eating capabilities, the Piranha is distributed widely throughout tropical South America. This large shoaling fish will grow to around 12 in (30cm) if given enough food and space. It cannot be kept with other species, and only young specimens are suitable for the home aquarium. Handle with care at all times.

Trichogaster leeri
Pearl Gourami
This Gourami from Southeast Asia has attractive and striking markings. A hardy, mild-mannered fish, it grows to around 6 in (15cm) long and can cope with most water types.

Trichogaster microlepis
Moonlight Gourami
Also known as the Moonbeam Gourami, this silver-blue fish from Thailand and Cambodia is typically peaceful and retiring. It grows to about 5 in (13cm) and prefers slightly acidic water.

Trichogaster trichopsis
Lavender Gourami
This attractive variant has shimmering blue to purple coloring and, like the species type, distinctive pelvic fins elongated into long sensory filaments.

Trichogaster trichopterus var.
Gold Gourami
Dark wavy markings on the dorsal surface and red and yellow speckled fins mark out this aquarium-bred hybrid. It grows to around 5 in (13cm) in length, and prefers soft water.

Trichopsis pumilus
Sparkling Gourami
This attractive, small Gourami with bright blue eyes and clear fins comes from Southeast Asia. A peaceful fish, it prefers slightly acidic water in a community tank.

Xiphophorus helleri var.
Green Swordtail
The wild strain of this distinctive aquarium-bred fish originates from Guatemala and Mexico. Very hardy, and easy to breed, it can grow to 4 in (10cm) or more.

Xiphophorus helleri var.
Gold Comet Swordtail
Named for the comet-like streaks at the top and bottom of the tail fin, this is one of a number of colorful strains that have been bred from the Central American progenitor. Note that only males have the caudal fin extension.

Xiphophorus helleri var.
Red Swordtail
This distinctive fish from Mexico, a colored form of the Green Swordtail, is hardy enough to withstand most water types.

Xiphophorus maculatus var.
Blue Coral Platy
There are over 40 different Platy hybrids, most of which are well suited to community tanks. For best results, place in medium-hard water, with no added salt. Transfer pregnant females to a separate tank to gestate.

Xiphophorus maculatus var.
Neon Blue Platy
Like other Platy, this popular aquarium fish is hardy and easy to breed. It tends to prefer a community tank with slightly alkaline water.

Xiphophorus maculatus var.
Red Platy
This red strain of the Platy prefers patches of dense vegetation in community tanks. For best results, place in medium-hard, slightly alkaline water.

Xiphophorus maculatus var.
Yellow Platy
This bold, brightly colored little fish is one of the many beautiful variants of the Platy. It prefers medium-hard, slightly alkaline water in the aquarium.

Xiphophorus variatus var.
High-Fin Platy
A stream-dweller from northeastern Mexico, this beautiful species is found in many color variations. The male grows to 1½ in (4cm), with the female slightly larger. It prefers slightly alkaline water.

plant directory

Acorus gramineus
Fountain Plant

This small but
striking plant
has dark green,
spiky leaves that
are elongated
and very slender.
The leaves come
from a central point
and protrude out of the center of the plant.
Very grass-like in appearance, this plant
prefers neutral water and moderate light.

Alternanthera rosaefolia

This extremely attractive plant has the
deepest red coloration of any aquatic
species. The spear-shaped leaves range in
color from dark maroon to pink and
can grow up to 3 in (7.5cm)
long. They are carried on
multibranched woody
stems. *Alternanthera* has
a reputation as a difficult
plant to grow, largely because
it needs a very strong light
source to thrive. It should be
planted in bunches of 4 to 6
stems in middle- or background.

Anubias nana
Dwarf Anubias

Dwarf Anubias is a
small, attractive bog plant
from central Africa. Carried on dainty
stems, the tough, waxy, elliptical or egg-
shaped leaves grow to around 2 in (5cm) in
length. It prefers neutral or slightly soft
water but tolerates a range of water types
as long as the substrate is rich in nutrients.

Aponogeton undulatus

With its translucently bright to dark green,
wavy edged leaves, this Sri Lankan native
is among the most beautiful of aquatic
plants. It can reach a height of 18 in
(45cm) and is therefore excellent for middle
ground use in the aquarium. The plant
prefers a nutrient-rich substrate with clay,
but adapts quite easily to the environment
in most aquariums. It
produces an emergent
spike with white or
cream colored flowers
that can be artificially
pollinated with a fine brush.
Alternatively, *Aponogeton
undulatus* can be reproduced by
simply dividing the tuberous
rootstock.

Bacopa caroliniana
Baby Tears

This American native plant is semi-aquatic
but grows well submerged. It has long
stems which can reach 12 in (30cm) in
height. The small, fleshy, pale green leaves
may acquire a reddish tinge in bright light.
These plants need
no special water
conditions and can
be easily propagated
by nipping off the
tips of the stems
and planting them
in the gravel. Plants
should be planted in
bunches of four to
five.

Cabomba aquatica var.
Green Cabomba

From both North and South America, this old
aquarium favorite with finely divided leaves
is also known as Fanwort
Cabomba is an excellent
oxygenator and has
feather-like leaves
that create a
dramatic
display in the
tank. The
leaves are
normally green
but can also be
reddish in color. The
Cabomba needs strong
light and prefers slightly
acidic water.

Cabomba aquatica var.
Red Cabomba

This red variant of *C. aquatica* has similar
finely divided leaves carried on opposite
pairs on long thin stems. The frond-
like leaves act as
unintentional
filters, picking
up floating debris,
and soon look
untidy unless good
filtration is provided in
the tank.

Ceratopteris thalicroides
Indian Fern

This beautiful fern from
Asia and Africa has soft,
pale green fronds which are
deeply subdivided. It
prefers strong light and
grows rapidly in soft,
slightly acidic water.

Chlorophytum bichetti
Wheat Plant

Striking and bold, this slender
bog plant is common
throughout northern Europe.
Its long, thin, variegated leaves
grow straight out of the gravel.
While not happy submerged for
weeks at a time, it can look
good for short periods
underwater.

Cryptocoryne blassii

A striking plant bearing narrow ovate
leaves with acute bases and bluntly pointed
tips. The leaf surface may be smooth or
puckered, and
range in color
from olive-
green to wine-red,
with a reddish
underside. This makes a
fine background plant for large aquariums,
or an equally good centerpiece in a smaller
tank. It is found growing on limestone, and
tolerates hard water well.

Cryptocoryne ciliata

This plant has a vast natural range, from
eastern India to Thailand, and on to
Indonesia, and as a result has produced
several distinct varieties. Tolerant of all
water types, it thrives on iron-rich clay and
once established will grow quickly to 20 in
(50cm) if given the space.

Cryptocoryne wendtii

This aquarium plant from Southeast Asia
has elongated, tough leaves colored mid-
green to deep olive, although some red or
purple tinged varieties are also available.
This plant grows best in
partial shade and
thrives in soft,
acidic water,
although it will
tolerate most
conditions. It will
grow in thick
clumps up to about
8 in (20cm) in
height.

Dracaena sanderiana
Green Dracena

This attractive plant
from Southeast Asia
has dark green,
pointed leaves
on soft fleshy
stems. It
generally prefers
medium-hard,
neutral water.

Dracaena sanderiana var.
Red and White Dracena

Similar to the Green Dracena, this
plant has pointed
leaves on soft
stems. It has a
very attractive red
tinge to the edges of
the leaves and stems.

Echinodorus magdalensis
Dwarf Amazon Sword Plant

This miniature version of the Amazon
Sword Plant grows to around 4 in (10cm)
high and has thin, pretty leaves. It is
tolerant of all water types and can quickly
form a large clump along
the bottom of the
aquarium.

Echinodorus tenellus
Pygmy Chain Sword Plant
With a natural distribution from the southern U.S. to Brazil, this plant has several distinct growing forms. The standard variety reaches a height of 6 in (15cm) but there are both smaller and larger types. It can spread quickly to form an attractive, dense grass-like carpet across the gravel in the tank, and prefers neutral to slightly acidic water.

Eleocharis acicularis
Hairgrass
This attractive North American bog plant grows to about 6 in (15cm) in height and spreads due to its creeping roots, producing new plants under the gravel. Hairgrass prefers moderate or bright light and slightly acidic water conditions. Its thin long leaves look like grass.

Giant Red Ivy
With their three-pronged leaves and thick stems, these reddish-tinged marsh plants add an attractive appearance to the aquarium. Like Arrowhead, it is happiest when not submerged for long periods of time and so is best used as extra foliage in the dry section of a wet-and-dry tank.

Hygrophila polysperma
Water Star
Also known as Dwarf Hygrophila, this popular plant comes from Southeast Asia. The thin stems hold bunches of small, blunt-tipped leaves which can grow very rapidly if the aquarium conditions are right. The plant prefers strong light and normal water conditions.

Lobelia cardinalis
Red lobelia
This small and pretty plant has a light red tinge to the leaves and forms a small clump. A garden plant rather than an aquatic, it is best not kept submerged for long periods of time.

Ludwigia repens
Red Ludwigia
This plant is native to northern Europe and has long, thin stems with small diamond-shaped leaves. It is usually green but in strong light the leaves develop a red tinge. The stems are grown in small clump.

Myriophyllum aquaticum
From North and Central America, this is a striking variation of the Water Milfoil plant. The thin stems carry clusters of 2 in (5cm) long olive-green to red leaves, the exact color depending on the level of illumination. This plant requires clean, clear water and needs to be pruned.

Nitella
This distinctive plant produces whorls of very fine leaves on long, curving, slender stems. Liable to become too leggy, they are best used as a temporary measure until other plants become established.

Nomaphila stricta
Giant Indian Water Star
Also known as *Giant Hygrophila*, this plant comes from Southeast Asia. It produces dark green, almond-shaped leaves on long, woody stems, and can have beautiful blue-purple, flowers if the stems reach the water level.

Sagittaria terres
Dwarf Sagittaria
This plant is common throughout northern Europe and produces bright green, strap- like leaves. It provides plenty of oxygen and grows very rapidly. It tends to prefer hard water with moderate light.

Selag wildenowii
Umbrella Fern
This tropical marsh fern from Africa has dark green leaves. It is not an easy plant to grow, but appears to do best in more subdued lighting conditions.

Spathiphyllum wallisii
A perennial plant from Sri Lanka with deep green, narrow, undulating leaves. Although it may start rather small, it grows quickly to about 10 in (25cm) in height in the aquarium. This elegant plant appears to thrive in corners where waste tends to pile up—the plant benefits from such good nourishment and plenty of light.
S. wallisii can be kept in all water conditions.

Syngonium podophyllum
Arrowhead
Also known as Crow Foot or Goose Foot, this attractive bog plant has deeply lobed leaves with three large prongs. It is available in both green and variegated types. It can be kept submerged for short periods of time.

Synnema triflorum
Water Wisteria
This pretty plant from India and Malaysia can become rather untidy. It has finely divided, feathery leaves which are pale green and very brittle. It grows best in soft water with bright light.

Vallisneria spiralis
Straight Vallis
This elegant Vallis is found in most tropical areas and spreads rapidly to form dense clumps. It grows best near a strong light source but is indifferent to water quality. Vallis is a good oxygenator and has long, thin leaves that can grow up to 15 in (38cm).

Vallisneria tortifolia
Twisted Vallis
Also known as Corkscrew Vallis, this tropical plant has very long, thin leaves that twist attractively as they rise. The leaves can grow to 15 in (38cm) long. It is best kept in strong light where it will grow into thick clumps.

index

credits

Quarto would like to thank and acknowledge the following suppliers and retailers, who generously loaned materials and equipment for photography:

A1 Laboratory Suppliers, UK
Tel: +44 (0)20 8850 0907/8
Fax: +44 (0)20 8859 6026

Fred Aldous Ltd, UK
Tel: +44 (0)161 2364224
Fax: +44 (0)161 2366075
www.safestreet.co.uk/fredaldous

Armitage Pet Care, UK
Tel: +44 (0)115 9381200
Fax: +44 (0)115 963124
http://www.armitages.co.uk

The Fossil Store, UK
Tel/Fax: +44 (0)1772 200258

Rolf C. Hagen (UK) Ltd
Tel: +44 (0)1977 556622
Fax: +44 (0)1977 513465
www.hagen.com

James Hetley & Co. Ltd, UK
Tel: +44 (0)20 7780 2345
Fax: +44 (0)20 7790 2682
www.hetleys.co.uk

Hidden Earth
Tel/Fax: +44 (0)1666 577506

Humbrol Limited, UK
Tel: +44 (0)1482 701191
Fax: +44 (0)1482 712908

Interpet Publishing, UK
Tel: +44 (0)1306 881033
Fax: +44 (0)1306 885009

Mineral Warehouse, UK
Tel: +44 (0)1903 877037
Fax: +44 (0)1903 877128
www.minware.co.uk

Presto Pets
Tel: +44 (0)1992 522599
Fax: +44 (0)1992 522559

Rainbow Rock Manufacturers, UK
Tel: +44 (0)29 2081 0663
Fax: +44 (0)29 2081 3519

Rosewood Pet Products Ltd., UK
Tel: +44 (0)1952 883408
Fax: +44 (0)1952 884359

Starline Aquatics, UK
Victoria House
3 Victoria Court
Hodgson Way
Wickford Business Park
Wickford
Essex SS11 8YY, UK

Travis Perkins Trading Company Limited,
UK
Tel: +44 (0) 20 7387 6079
Fax: +44 (0)20 7383 3068
www.travisperkins.co.uk

Special thanks to Dave Goodwin of Starline Aquatics, for supplying the tanks, fish, and many of the plants and other materials used in the photographs. We are especially grateful to him and his staff for their hospitality, advice, assistance, and endless patience during the photoshoots. The book would not have been possible without Dave's boundless knowledge of aquarium fish and their care.

Special thanks to Crucial Books, London.